Living Dangerously

COUNTERPOINTS

Studies in the Postmodern Theory of Education

Joe L. Kincheloe and Shirley R. Steinberg
General Editors

Vol. 1

PETER LANG
New York • San Francisco • Bern • Baltimore
Frankfurt am Main • Berlin • Wien • Paris

Henry A. Giroux

Living Dangerously

Multiculturalism and the Politics of Difference

PETER LANG
New York • San Francisco • Bern • Baltimore
Frankfurt am Main • Berlin • Wien • Paris

Library of Congress Cataloging-in-Publication Data

Giroux, Henry A.
    Living dangerously : multiculturalism and the politics
of difference/ Henry A. Giroux.
    p.cm. — (Counterpoints: Studies in the Postmodern
Theory of Education ; vol. 1)
        1. Critical pedagogy—United States.
2. Education—Political aspects—United States.
3. Pluralism (Social sciences)—United States.
4. Education—United States—Philosophy. I. Title.
II. Series.
LC196.5.U6G57 1993   370.19'0973—dc20   93–20107
ISBN 0-8204-1832-3   CIP
ISSN 1058-1634

Cover design by James F. Brisson.

The painting on the front cover entitled "Night of the
Living Dead" by William Turner is reproduced by the
kind permission of the artist.

Die Deutsche Bibliothek—CIP—Einheitsaufnahme

Giroux, Henry A.:
Living dangerously: multiculturalism and the politics of
difference / Henry A. Giroux.—New York; Bern; Berlin;
Frankfurt/M.; Paris; Wien: Lang, 1993
    (Counterpoints ; Vol. 1)
    ISBN 0-8204-1832-3
NE: GT

The paper in this book meets the guidelines for permanence and
durability of the Committee on Production Guidelines for
Book Longevity of the Council on Library Resources.

© Peter Lang Publishing, Inc., New York 1993

Printed in the United States of America.

To Toni Morrison,
who knows that love, courage, desire and possibility
hang out in the most unlikely places.

"I envy them their public love. I myself have only known it in secret, shared it in secret and longed, longed to show it-to be able to say out loud what they have no need to say at all: That I have loved only you, surrendered my whole self reckless to you and nobody else. That I want you to love me back and show it to me. That I love the way you hold me, how close you let me be to you. I like your fingers on and on, lifting, turning. I have watched your face for a long time now, and missed your eyes when you went away from me. Talking to you and hearing you answer--that's the kick." (Toni Morrison, **Jazz**, 1992, p. 229.)

Table of Contents

Preface

As a small boy growing up in the Smith Hill section of Providence, Rhode Island, I made spending money shining shoes on Thursday, Friday, and Saturday nights. I used to frequent mostly Black night clubs along a two mile strip about a mile from my family's third floor rented apartment. I can still remember walking into a world filled with blues, jazz, smoke, dance, and on a few occasions witnessed Fats Domino and other big name stars pounding away at the club's piano. I also remember constantly being hassled by kids in the neighborhood who tried to steal the money I made. I hated to fight, but I had to learn fast how to negotiate a borderland crisscrossed with the complexity of race, class, and violence. Soon I became friends with a group of working class white & Black kids and we went into "business" together. We carved out a territory to shine shoes, arranged places for crap games, decided what trucks could come into the neighborhood to sell fruits. And none of us ever dreamed of going to Stanford or Harvard University. At night we broke into gyms and played until the sweat drenched our bodies and the basketball seemed to shrink in size because we pounded it against the floor and backboard so much. We always knew we were on the border. We knew it when the cops came by and threw their billy clubs at our legs, when the college students walked by our street corner and looked away to avert our stares born of territorial rights and hard fought turf wars, and we recognized how class differences were lived out through privileges we didn't care to participate in at the time. Somewhere Gramsci mentions that our lives consists of traces that we need to take an inventory of once and awhile. This book is dedicated to the traces that have always made me aware of where I come from and what it meant to live dangerously, and to know that one can never be alone with such memories.

Acknowledgments

Acknowledgements have become the new markers indicating webs of association that place one in the pantheon of "respected" company. I refuse this trite exercise. I simply want to thank my friends Peter McLaren, Donaldo Macedo, Carol Becker, Michael Dyson, Roger I. Simon, Candy Mitchell, Paulo Freire, Jeanne Brady, Stanley Aronowitz, Lech Witkowski, Larry Grossberg, Harvey Kaye, Ava Collins, Joe Kincheloe, Joe Kretovics, Shirley R. Steinberg, Pat Shannon, Priscilla Ross, and Cleo Cherryholmes who always combine humility and insight with a passion for dialogue and living dangerously. A sincere thanks goes to my former graduate students at Miami University who struggled with their dreams, ruptured the pretense of innocence, and renounced the comforts of careers made through attacks on others more established than themselves. They always knew that real problems were somewhere other than in the academic journals or well publicized symposiums. Indeed, their visions and hopes presaged a future with justice while demanding a concerted struggle with the past and present. I will miss them. Thanks to Honor Fagan, Martin O'Neill, Stephen Haymes, Adriana

Hernandez, Susan Searls, David Trend, Tom Szkuldarek, Marjorie Roemer, Vandana Sharma, Barry Nedelman, Tom Oldenski, Khaula Murtadha, and Suellyn Hanke.

Revised versions of some of these chapters have appeared in *The Review of Education, Cultural Studies*, Jim Collins, et. al., eds., *Film Theory Goes to the Movies* (Routledge, 1992); Henry A. Giroux, "Educational Leadership and the Crisis of Democratic Government," *Educational Researcher*, 21 (4) 1992, pp. 4-11. Copyright 1992 by the American Educational Research Association. Adapted by permission of the publisher. Giroux, H.A. 1992 "Language, Difference and Curriculum Theory: Beyond the Politics of Clarity," *Theory Into Practice*, 31 (3) (219-227.) (Theme issue on "Grounding Contemporary Curriculum Thought.") Copyright 1992 College of Education, The Ohio State University.

Henry A. Giroux
State College
January 1993

Introduction

by Joe L. Kincheloe

The Los Angeles insurrection of April 1992 provided a compelling camera angle on George Bush's New World Order. Rodney King's Simi Valley jurors pronouncements on equality under the law and their concomitant color blindness alerted the attentive to a new form of racial discrimination that was somehow different than the old-fashioned racism of bygone days. It is Henry Giroux's charge in this volume to explain the dynamics which have helped create both the nihilistic urban landscape on which the L.A. drama unfolded and the ideological frame in which the King jurors and millions of other American could miss, or dismiss, the racial dimensions of the Rodney King case. Giroux introduces us to the role of pedagogy in the New World Order, as he explores the nature of the new racism. George Bush is correct about one thing: There is a New World Order. However, it may not be the apocalyptic one that he wanted. Maintaining hope as he describes the despair of the oppressed within this new order, Giroux transcends the modernist boundaries of national loyalty drawing upon the work of such eclectic theorists as Ernesto LaClau, Chantal Mouffe, Paulo Friere, Nancy Fraser, and John Dewey.

As the title implies, this is a book about living dangerously, about civic courage and the form it might take on the multicellular terrain of the late twentieth century. Giroux envisions the possibility of an education grounded on an ethic of risk that is unafraid to expose the mutations of racism and the ways in which such social forms work to undermine the democratic impulse in postmodern life. In many ways the book is a *Democracy and Education Redux;* not in an imitative sense, but in a way that understands John Dewey's relationship to the world in 1916 and expands that cognizance to the hyperreality of the 1990s. Aware of Dewey's unparalleled pedagogical brilliance, Giroux nonetheless negotiates theoretical curves Dewey could not have imagined. Exploring a world that Dewey would have thought conceivable only by a Jules Verne, Giroux moves educational theory to the postmodern domain.

In this context, Giroux develops a democratic pedagogy for both the governors and the governed. The notion of leadership prevalent in Bush's New World Order revolves around the demands of the market place and the corporation. Removed from ethical responsibility, such leadership avoids questions of power, culture, and identity. Attempting to transcend a discourse of sterile technicism, Giroux envisions educational leaders as intellectuals who decipher codes of power while extending visions of possibility to the dispossessed. Unafraid of the political functions of leadership, Giroux's leaders take democracy seriously as they learn to challenge the prevalent "money and missiles" form of reality. The postmodern democratic leader refuses to honor only traditions that validate "the existent," choosing instead to understand leadership as a form of moral activity and social criticism.

As he explores the relationship between democracy and education, Giroux constructs his view of both educational leaders and teachers around the notion of cultural workers. Too often, he argues, we have viewed cultural work for democracy as the domain of only artists, writers and media producers. Teachers who are cultural workers strive to minimize the oppression which afflicts the lives of their students and fellow teachers.   Giroux's concept of critical citizenship moves far beyond the conservative flag waving variety which fails to examine the values which inform citizenship.   The critical citizen in the postmodern world, Giroux asserts, attempts to encourage maximum political unity without denying difference. *America 2000* speaks of responsible citizenship but avoids any serious discussion of how educators might negotiate the relationship among schooling, democracy, and the education of citizens.   When citizenship is mentioned by those in power in the 1990s it is typically limited to a negative concept--a form of activity which is confined to a rule-following rewarded by freedom from state interference.   In schools, questions of citizenship education remain within this context, as good citizenship is equated with high test scores, not with complex questions about what kind of citizens and society we want and the kinds of values they possess.   Critical citizenship education moves far beyond the passive learning of specific rights.   Echoing Dewey early in the century, Giroux claims that democratic citizenship education involves actives participation in the life of the public.

The language Giroux uses to address questions of democracy and citizenship has always been a major issue for his readers.   It will remain at the center of controversy in the critiques of this book. Giroux creates a new language of pedagogy, a language which will serve as a wake-up call for sleeping educators.   Maintaining that new socio-political conditions demand new languages, he writes of a pedagogy of representation and a pedagogy of place.   Refusing to treat teachers as incapable of dealing with complexity, Giroux engages a form of writing which does not simply translate a reality "out there" in some sort of positivistic notion of correspondence.   Instead he provides a language of theory and complexity which encourages the creation of a new reality.   Languages of simplistic correspondence fail to provide an awareness of one's biographical, ideological, and historical situatedness.   And without such an awareness both readers and writers fail to understand the ways subjects are produced, the ways our consciousness are constructed.   Without such appreciations, the ability to escape the ideology of the New World Order and to become a cultural worker for democracy is severely limited.

As Giroux develops his new language of a postmodern era, he transgresses traditional boundaries in the process of redefining pedagogy. Overcoming the tyranny of technicist definitions involving the unexamined transmission of data from one party to another, Giroux conceives pedagogy as a form of cultural work which involves the production of knowledge and social identities. In a postmodern hyperreality, critical pedagogy must be concerned with representations and the way they produce meanings. The nature of these representations and the meanings they produce are central to the project of democracy. Return for a moment to the Los Angeles insurrection. The way in which the poor black community of South Central Los Angeles has been represented shapes the way North American and Europeans come to see the politics of the issues. For example, if we accept the right-wing representation of the Black and Hispanic residents of L.A. as lazy welfare cheaters with a natural predisposition to violence, we are far more likely to favor forceful solutions to the "law and order problem in Los Angeles" than if we understand the insidious nature of neo-racism.

Giroux maintains that conservative forces have expended great energy in the struggle over the control of the popular media and other spheres of representation to shape racial meanings and to connect racial representations to larger political and cultural agendas. In this context, Giroux presents his pedagogy of representation. Giroux's students study not only the various ways that representations are shaped and inscribed, but how they come to question the political, historical, and semiotic dynamics that produce the larger regimes of representation responsible for shaping individual lives, schools, and society. As they study these representations and dynamics, students analyze the historical situatedness of particular forms of representation, deploy a variety of critical methodologies to discern how certain textual representations shape identity, and ask whose interests are served by specific representations. Thus, the pedagogy of representation becomes an act of resistance and transformation, as students develop the ability to challenge the representations that foster racism, sexism, and colonialism. A central struggle on the postmodern educational landscape involves the representation of the legacies of dominant cultural expressions as well as attempts to challenge and rewrite them. It is over these representations that contemporary debates over multiculturalism are waged.

This book breaks new ground as Giroux displays his engaging and innovative pedagogical techniques, his pedagogy of the popular. Often criticized for not linking theory to practice, Giroux presents a pedagogy which deconstructs and reclaims various aspects of popular culture in a way which challenges canonicity, rejects a view of identity as a privatized consciousness, and refuses to validate the idea that cultural difference is a threat to democracy. In this work, Giroux analyzes various popular films including *Dead Poets Society*, *Stand and Deliver*, and *Grand Canyon*, in the process opening a dialogue on the issues of difference, identity and democracy in light of the politics of representation. Unlike educators of the past, Giroux avoids the pitfalls of "relevance" which have often eventuated in three anti-emancipatory outcomes: 1.) Television and popular culture are used to make the Eurocentric canon seem more relevant; 2.) A decontextualized use of popular culture attempts to make a boring school experience more interesting, avoiding the critical questioning of texts and the lived world of students; 3.) The concern for relevance smothers democratic impulses and concerns for social justice. Aware of such possibilities, Giroux's pedagogy of the popular connects the content of student identity formation to issues of democracy, representation and difference, while at the same time students gain a new passion for the educational process.

The soul of *Living Dangerously* involves the reconceptualization of multicultural education around the issues of democracy, identity politics and difference. Tired of liberal portrayals of multiculturalism conceived outside of a political context and divorced from a concern with the effect of power relations on self-production and racial identity, Giroux pushes educators to embrace democracy in the contemporary debate over multiculturalism, to frame multiculturalism as a democratic discourse. The successful right-wing attack on multiculturalism and the culturally-different is not only the most serious issue facing Blacks, Hispanics, and Native Americans, but it threatens the survival of democracy itself. George Bush's attempt to bind schools to the logic of the marketplace diminished the importance of democracy in both academic and public life. Americans in the 1990s are no longer moved by the political. The same thing that inspired the workers and students in Poland, Czechoslovakia, and China to lay their lives on the line for democracy is no longer very important to domesticated American youth or to the larger public. The Charlottesville Education Summit and Bush's *America 2000* illustrate this retreat from democracy as they separate equity from excellence and social responsibility. The idea of schools extending or reconstructing democratic public life is simply unimportant to the architects of national educational policy. It is as if Dewey and the work he did have been erased from American history. Giroux calls our attention to the fact that George Bush as a democratic emperor was naked. Surrounded by his storm troopers of representation who inscribed him as tough, but kind and gentle, Bush and his cohorts chipped away at the educational, legal, institutional, and ideological spheres essential to the perpetuation of democracy.

Drawing upon post-structuralist and feminist insights, Giroux connects identity politics to his larger concern with multiculturalism and the struggle for democracy. Modernist forms of identity ignored how individual subjectivity was constructed within complex and contradictory social formations. Individuals in this context were independent and autonomous, blessed with a simple free will to make rational choices. Free from the constraints of domination and unburdened by history, the modernist subject traveled freely on the political landscape. Giroux's notion of identity politics challenges this modernist simplicity, as it promotes a pedagogy of place, an educational strategy which demands that we become self-conscious of our own historical locations. Contrary to charges of critics who claim that he operates within the frames of unexamined master narratives, Giroux suggests that educators examine the forces that shape them whether they be neo-conservatives or critical pedagogues. Such an ability becomes a democratic survival skill on the urban postmodern landscape with its multiple forms of identity construction. A pedagogy of place becomes an armor against the right wing representational tyranny which seeks to maintain the inequitable power relations of the status quo. Seeing identity politics as a new and threatening bogeyman, right wing politicians have attempted to respond to the assertive posture of Blacks, Hispanics, homosexuals and women by representing them outside the political dynamics which created the power asymmetries which plague them. Thus, democratic egalitarian impulses are held in check, the subversive tendencies of difference are contained.

As he discusses the relationship between difference and the struggle for democracy, Giroux demarcates the dissimilarities between the old racism and the representations of neo racism. The old racism was grounded on the superiority of whites and the presentation of Anglo European culture as the definition of civilization. The new racism views difference not as a marker of racial superiority, but as a sign for cultural containment, monoculturalism, and socioeconomic inequality. Paraded under a banner of nationalism and patriotism this racist notion of cultural uniformity flies under the cultural radar, the national consciousness of the anti-democratic nature of racism. In the postmodern world of neo-racism, Whites are represented as the victims of racial inequality. They are denied jobs because of workplaces which favor "incompetent" minorities. They are denied admission to professional schools because of admission policies which favor "less qualified" minorities and they are excluded from cities because of the racism of "violent" minorities. Unlike the old racism, neo-racism always allows its perpetrators the right of plausible deniability. After all, George Bush claimed to stand tough against racism of all forms.

One of the reasons that recent denunciations of racism from the left have exerted so little effect is that they have failed to account for this mutation in the nature of racism, this change in the way difference is constituted. Giroux insightfully uncovers an ostensible paradox in the right-wing politics of difference. Conservatives promote racial difference as a significant aspect of American life and, at the same time, a threat to be overcome. Giroux tells us that these strategies are not in conflict with one another. In the first place, the right-wing promotes racial difference for the purpose of mobilizing the anxieties of Whites into a political constituency for larger political goals. Secondly, the right-wing attacks racial difference as a malignancy to be removed. In this context conservatives call for standardized tests, attack multiculturalism as an assault on national unity and employ an acontextual notion of cultural pluralism to display and contain difference without awakening the dangerous concepts of power and oppression. Decontextualized difference, Giroux argues, has been used as an effective right-wing weapon against the expansion of democracy. We do not need a common culture, he concludes, just a common ground for dialogue.

This dialogue might begin around the question of what it means to be white in North America. My white students come to class with little concept of their own ethnicity. The have been dehistoricized, abstracted from their pasts and the social construction of their consciousness. Giroux contends that we must make whiteness visible as an ethnic category. In the present era, whiteness is simply not understood in the context of social relations that evoke privilege or power. It is this type of task, the historical and political contextualization of whiteness that informs the project of a critical pedagogy. This is Giroux at his best: the critical educational theorist who assesses the complex and ever-changing ways in which identities are produced. As has been argued in increasingly sophisticated ways over the last fifteen years, an education which is critical creates situations where students find it possible to assume subject positions grounded on the principles of equality, justice, and freedom.

This volume initiates a publishing project with great promise. Peter Lang Publishing's commitment to a series of books which explore the cutting edge of critical postmodern theory and its relationship to education marks a valuable advance in our field. Giroux's title, *Living Dangerously*, captures the spirit of this series as it refuses the safety and comfort of the mainstream. As the work has changed, so too must educational thought and practice. We thank Henry Giroux and the other authors in the series for their visions of what can be. Also, we thank Michael Flamini, senior editor at Peter Lang, for his excellent editorial work and his commitment to the idea of this series.

1.

Education, Leadership and the Crisis of a Democratic Culture

I want to draw upon two recent events that, while appearing slightly removed from the related issues of leadership and schooling, provide a constructive starting point for developing a new language that might raise fresh questions about what it means to educate students for forms of leadership which will expand the visions and vistas that animate democratic public life.[1]

The first event is the remarkable changes that have taken place in Eastern Europe and the Soviet Union within the last few years. We have witnessed the fall of the Berlin Wall. Stalinist Communist parties have been overthrown throughout Eastern Europe, and the Soviet Union, beset by a nationalist fervor, has reconstituted itself as a series of independent republics. We live in an age in which a radical conception of leadership has emerged that is wedded to the construction of a new political subject. This is a political subject who appears to reject the authoritarianism of master narratives; refuses traditions which allow only for reverence of what already is; denies those instrumental and universalized forms of rationality which eliminate the historical and the contingent; refuses to subordinate the discourse of ethics to the politics of verification; and recognizes a substantive citizenship which requires a multiple subject who can speak and act as a critical and responsible citizen in a variety of settings. Such a subject links freedom not merely to individual rights but to a comprehensive theory of human welfare.

The second event to which I am referring was a remarkable series of articles entitled "The Trouble with Politics" that ran in the March 1990 issue of the *New York Times*.   Using the occasion of Czechoslovakian President Vaclav Havel's address before a joint session of Congress, the *Times* articles boldly suggested that whatever it is that motivated workers, intellectuals, and students in Poland, Czechoslovakia and China to risk their lives for democracy no longer inspired American youth or the larger public. Stressing the importance of politics and ethics to democracy, the *Times* articles implicitly raised the issue of how crucial the theory and practice of leadership is in keeping alive a conception of democracy as an ideal filled with possibilities richly deserved but never guaranteed: in this case, an ideal that can only be understood as part of a broader and incessant struggle for freedom and human dignity. For Havel, democracy, in the full sense of the word, is an end point that one moves steadily toward without ever reaching. As Peter Euben points out, "We steadily move toward it while recognizing that there is no finality to the goal that nonetheless guides us; the distance between it and ourselves mandates that we treat every means as an end and every end as a means...that we add depth to central terms of our political discourse: democracy, power, freedom, and politics....by taking seriously Lincoln's belief that government is rightly of, by, and for the people."[2] The *Times* articles not only highlighted the importance of democracy as a powerful script for human freedom, they also made visible the inability of the American public to grasp the full significance of its own indifference to the need to struggle for the conditions that make democracy a substantive, rather than lifeless, activity.

At all levels of national and daily life, the breadth and depth of democratic relations are being rolled back. This is seen for example, in

the rising apathy expressed in the refusal of eligible voters to participate in national elections (45.5 percent of the potential electorate did
not vote in the 1992 Presidential election, statistics indicative of a
democracy that has become dysfunctional), the systematic transfer of
wealth from the poor to the rich, the ongoing attacks by the government and courts on civil rights and the welfare system, and the prolif-
erating incidents of racist harassment and violence on college and public school sites. The eclipse of the discourse of public life can be seen
in a growing sentiment that "dismisses morality and human rights as a
leftover from bygone days."[3]

The retreat from democracy is also evident in the absence of
serious talk about how as a nation we might educate future generations
in the language and practice of moral compassion, critical agency, and
the utopian horizons of social imagination. The discourse of leadership
appears trapped in a vocabulary in which the estimate of a good society
is expressed in indices that measure markets, defense systems, and the
Gross National Product. Missing in this discourse is a vocabulary for
talking about and creating democratic public cultures and communities
that are attentive to the problems of homelessness, hunger, censorship,
media manipulation, and the rampant individualism and greed that conservative political commentator, Kevin Phillips, claims has become the
hallmark of the last decade.[4] I believe that the contrasts between the
struggle for democracy in Eastern Europe and its declining significance
in American life posits a major challenge for defining a notion of leadership that would place schools of education in the forefront of this
country's attempt to address the urgent need to create prospective administrators and teachers as engaged intellectuals motivated by a vision
capable of defending and assisting in the survival of the United States
as a vibrant, democratic society. Throughout this chapter, I use the
term democracy and democratic society. Both terms, in this case, are
linked to citizenship understood as a form of self-management constituted in all major economic, social, and cultural spheres of society.
Democracy in this context takes up the issue of transferring power
from elites and executive authorities, who control the economic and
cultural apparatuses of society, to those producers who wield power at
the local level. At stake here is making democracy concrete through the

organization and exercise of horizontal power in which knowledge must be widely shared, through education and other technologies of culture. At issue here is recognizing that democracy is not merely about the formality of voting but more substantively about having access to the technological and cultural resources necessary to be informed, make decisions, and to exercise control over the material and ideological forces that govern peoples' lives. I believe that this question of democracy and citizenship occupies the center of an emancipatory project designed to educate students to the expanding claims of needs, rights, and obligations that are increasingly being promoted by new social groups and movements such as feminists, black and ethnic movements, ecology activists, gay and lesbian groups, and vulnerable minorities such as children and the aged. Democratic education in this instance would address the central question of membership in a community about who does and does not belong; it would provide opportunities for students to learn not only the rights but also the responsibilities needed to sustain a democratic notion of public life. As such, it would not be enough to call for a closer link between the school curriculum and community. What is also needed is the opportunity for students to perform a public service that allows them to take up the issue and practice of social reform as part of a broader attempt to identify and ameliorate, through collective struggle, forms of inequality and human suffering.[5]

In what follows, I want to emphasize the significance educational leadership has for addressing some of the issues and problems schools of education need to consider with respect to the social responsibility of school administrators and teachers and the role that both public schools and higher education might have in terms of their wider political and social function. My focus is not on management but on what it means to educate people capable of a vision, people who can rewrite the narrative of educational administration and the story of leadership by developing a public philosophy capable of animating a democratic society. At the outset, I want to reemphasize the fundamental importance of recognizing that democracy is not simply a lifeless tradition or disciplinary subject that is merely passed on from one generation to the next. Neither is democracy an empty set of regulations and procedures that can be subsumed in the language of proficiency, efficiency, and accountability. Nor is it an outmoded moral and political referent that simply makes governing more difficult in light of the rise of new rights and entitlements demanded by emerging social movements and groups. Put simply, democracy is both a discourse and a practice that produces particular narratives and identities in-the-making informed by the principles of freedom, equality, and social justice. It is expressed not in moral platitudes but in concrete struggles and practices that find expression in classroom social relations, everyday life, and memories of resistance and struggle. When wedded to its most emancipatory possibilities, democracy encourages all citizens to actively construct and share power over those institutions that govern their lives. At the same time the challenge of democracy resides in the necessary recognition that educators, parents, and others will have to work hard to insure that future generations will view the idea and practice of democracy as a goal worth believing in and struggling for.

Unfortunately, there is enormous evidence indicating that the related issues of democracy, leadership, and schooling are increasingly being incorporated as part of a reactionary political agenda. This agenda furthers the fortunes of narrow social interests that may be at odds with any emancipatory notion of substantive democracy. The discourse of American democracy has been appropriated and trivialized in bloated calls to force students to say the pledge of allegiance. It has been devalued and dismissed in dangerous reform proposals that pit a romanticized view of the laws and logic of the market against the discourse of ethics, political agency, and social responsibility. The concept of democracy has also come under fire with the rise of a new American nativism that calls for schools to be dispensers of an unproblematic cultural tradition in which the emergence of cultural difference is seen as a sign of fragmentation and a departure from rather than an advance towards democracy.

Current Educational Reform and the Crisis of American Democracy

The current debate about educating teachers and administrators represents more than a commentary on the state of public and higher education, it is fundamentally a debate about the relevance of democracy, social criticism, and critical thought to both our dreams and the stories that we devise in order to give meaning to our lives. This debate has taken a serious turn in the last decade and now as before its terms are being principally set by neo-liberals and conservatives. This can be seen in many of the current educational reform movements, particularly the Charlottesville Education summit of September 1989 and more recently the reform package set forth in *America 2000*. These movements embody a conception of educational leadership that generally ignores those closest to the schools such as superintendents, principals, teachers, students, and parents. As Joan Lipsitz points out reform movements such as *America 2000* also argue "by implication, that too many children of poverty now cannot gain access to the benefits of school's civil rights agendas....that policies set on behalf of equity are increasingly inequitable, and implicitly recommend policies that tolerate separatism."[6] I would argue that *America 2000*, in this case, must be called to task for developing policies that appear compatible with outright racist discrimination and segregation. These reforms present an agenda and a purpose for shaping public schooling and higher education in this country which abstract equity from excellence and social responsibility. Under the guise of attempting to revitalize the language of leadership and reform, these reports signify a dangerous attack on some of the most fundamental aspects of democratic public life and the social, moral, and political obligations of responsible, critical citizens. What has been valorized in this language is not the issue of reclaiming public schools or universities as agencies of social justice and critical democracy, but rather an elitist view of schooling based on a celebration of cultural uniformity, the reprivatization of public schools, an uncritical support for remaking school curricula in the interest of labor-market imperatives, and a return to the transmission model of teaching.

The growing threat to democracy, in this case, can also be seen in the attempt by the Reagan and Bush administrations to remove the idea of liberty from that of democracy, and to redefine citizenship not as part of a practice of rights and responsibilities towards a wider community, but as a sectarian arena of action dominated by the dictates of a narrow instrumentalism. Within this context, the sense of the public has become a negative prefix suggesting otherness, nurturance, community, morality, and other aspects of a social space that appear superfluous next to the imperatives of the market and its celebration of consumerism and self-interest. Understood as a form of self-management, "rights and responsibilities" constituted in all major economic, social, and cultural spheres of society, critical citizenship has become an unprofitable, if not subversive category.

Given the implications of the emerging attempts at educational reform for defining how administrators and teachers think of the practice of leadership and what this suggests for helping students imagine themselves as potential citizens of a democratic society, I want to comment briefly on some of the major features that characterize *America 2000* and its ideological alter ego, *Politics, Markets, and America's Schools* by John E. Chubb and Terry M. Moe.

America 2000 has put forth a notion of educational leadership and reform that is as significant for what it does not address as it is for the goals and programs it proposes. Organized around the imperatives of choice, standardized testing, and the reprivatization of public schools, it displays no sense of urgency in addressing the importance of schooling for improving the quality of democratic public life. Not only does it suffer from a curious form of historical amnesia by refusing to build on the gains of programs that have been quite successful in addressing the needs of children from subordinate groups (programs animated by models of educational leadership expressed in the work of Henry Levin, Deborah Meier, and James Comer), but it also has written out of its script some of the most pressing difficulties facing administrators and teachers in America's schools.[7] For instance, *America 2000* ignores such problems as child poverty at a time when 40% of all children are classified as poor;[8] it ignores the pressing problem of unemployment when the unemployment rate among black male teens in March 1991 was 38.4 percent. It ignores issues of health care, teen-age pregnancy, drugs, violence, and racial discrimination at a time when these issues play a central role in defining the quality of life for increasing numbers of students in this country. Instead of addressing how these issues impact upon schools, how they undermine how children learn, *America 2000* focuses instead on issues such as testing and choice. Testing runs the risk of becoming a code word for training educational leaders in the language of management, measurement, and efficiency. Testing has become the new ideological weapon in developing standardized curricula; a weapon that ignores how schools can serve populations of students that differ vastly with respect to cultural diversity, academic and economic resources, and classroom opportunities. The current infatuation with national testing shores up models of leadership wedded to the politics of not-naming, that is, a politics that ruthlessly expunges from its vocabulary how schools function through various sorting, administrative, and pedagogical processes to silence and marginalize teachers and students from developing curricula, locating themselves in their own histories, and speaking as subjects rather than as objects of educational reform.[9] There is no talk in this language of how the curriculum works to secure particular forms of authority. There is a disturbing silence in this perspective around the issue of who speaks, for whom, and under what conditions. Similarly, within this discourse of quantification and standardization there is little attention given to the issue of the relationship between knowledge and power. Missing are such questions as: What constitutes really useful knowledge? Whose interests does it serve? What kinds of social relations does it structure and at what price? How does school knowledge enable those who have been generally excluded from schools to speak and act with dignity?

In addition to the current emphasis on testing, school choice has become a fundamental element in the new educational reform movement. Choice is organized and developed according to the imperatives of the marketplace. Ignoring the primacy of the social, the current discourse on choice appeals to the logic of competitiveness, individualism, and achievement. While these attributes might sound plausible as fundamental elements in the logic of educational reform they are, in fact, used by neo-conservatives to develop a notion of educational leadership that undermines the responsibility of public service, ruptures the relationship between schools and the community, and diverts educators from the responsibility for improving education for all students in all schools. Choice is reduced to "privatization" and the idea that schools would be better off if they were operated in a 'free market'".[10] The choice proposals are at odds with providing diversity within schools that serve as neighborhood centers. Choice is not defined as a strategy to broaden the powers of teachers, students, and parents within neighborhood schools. On the contrary, within the educational discourse of reformers such as Chubb and Moe, choice is set against democracy, which is viewed as outdated, hopelessly complex and unsuited to the privileges of class, wealth, and cultural uniformity. Stuart Hall extends this critique by arguing that the notion of choice which structures mainstream educational reforms is marked by two fundamental weaknesses. He writes:

> The conception of choice which underpins [mainstream educational reforms]...assumes, as classic liberalism always has, that the means of exercising choice-money is evenly distributed. But the very market model on which it is based ensures that this cannot and never will be so. The granting of an equal right which only can be exercised unequally is a form of 'negative freedom'... The second [failure of the conservative notion of choice] is that modernity is more individuated but it is also more complex and thus more interdependent. Health, like transport, education, public amenities and a host of other things cannot be reduced in the modern world to an individual calculus.11

There is a disturbing implication in current reform agendas in the United States that as a society we have demanded *not too little, but too much* of democracy. Implicit in *America 2000* but more explicitly stated in *Politics, Markets, and American Schools*, is a dismissal of democracy as a political and moral referent for combining the capacity of individuals to pursue their own goals while simultaneously cultivating civic virtues that promote the public good.[12]   What is being refused in these reports is the urgent task of addressing forms of education that provide a democratic curriculum and culture that educates students as both individual subjects and as part of a democratic public culture. Rather than engaging the complex relationship between the twin logic of identity and freedom, on the one hand, and community and public responsibility on the other, the new right attempts to disarticulate democracy and citizenship from the principles of social justice, freedom, and equality. Within this discourse, citizenship is linked to a pedagogical practice that subordinates "all areas of life to the rule of the market and all democratic and intermediate institutions to the rule of the executive."[13]   Not only does such a discourse on leadership promote the exit of ethics and politics from schooling, but it offers little help in understanding how schools can contribute to a notion of citizenship regulated by the claims of social justice, equality, and community. In fact, the notion of choice and leadership that informs both *America 2000* and the work of Chubb and Moe is constructed around a limited picture of individual needs and consumer-driven desires which is fundamentally demeaning in its suggestion that the market expresses the paradigmatic view of human relations and what human beings could become.[14]

Current Educational Reforms and Conceptions of Leadership

The current infatuation with the marketplace can be seen in the support by mainstream educators and politicians of the view that leadership is to be modeled on the style and ideology of leading corporate executives. Former Secretary of Education, Lamar Alexander, selected David Kearns, former chief executive officer of the Xerox Corporation, as the nominee for Deputy Secretary of Education. Lee Iaccoca was mentioned as a serious candidate to run for the presidency of the United States. Pragmatism and the bottom line erase the memories and accomplishments of leaders such as Martin Luther King, Nelson Mandela, Robert Kennedy, and Vaclav Havel, who speak to a higher standard of leadership. In the meantime, *America 2000* calls upon prominent business leaders to both finance 535 new schools and to provide the prototype for other systems to emulate. Similarly, a central thrust for the current reform movement has been to forge a new alliance between the corporate sector and schools. In this case, the business of leadership narrows the relationship between democracy and freedom by leading schools down the path of corporate ethics and marketplace ideology. This becomes more clear as industry is increasingly called upon to intervene in local schools to provide teachers, advisors, curriculum materials, and other fundamental support and policy oriented services.

This view of educational leadership is disturbingly paradoxical. Not only does it ignore the language of community, solidarity, and the public good, it also draws unproblematically upon a sector of society that has given the American public the savings and loan scandals, the age of corporate buyouts, the proliferation of "junk" bonds, insider trading, and the large increase in white collar crime. It has also produced multinational corporate mergers that eliminate jobs and violate the public trust, and made leadership synonymous with the logic of the bottom line, self-interests, and corporate avarice. What is profoundly disturbing in this celebration of the alleged "free" market, as Robert Bellah and his associates have pointed out, is that it often rests on a "stubborn fear of acknowledging structures of interdependence in a technologically complex society dominated by giant corporations and an increasingly powerful state."[15] There is a strong propensity in this discourse and its attendant view of leadership to abstract leadership from ethical responsibility, to subordinate basic human needs to the narrow market measures, and to downplay the importance of creating support systems that name, address, and help students who are caught in the spiralling web of unemployment, poverty, racial discrimination, and institutional abuse.

This is not meant to suggest that questions of leadership and schooling should avoid engaging issues concerning work, economics, and the market place. What is essential here, especially for a reconstructed notion of leadership, is that a balance must be struck between institutions and public cultures that promote and cultivate human nurturance and those that "express the purely quantitative thinking of the market."[16]   While students need to learn the necessary skills and knowledge to qualify for decent employment, they also need to be literate in the discourse of economic and social justice.[17]   More importantly, the purpose and meaning of schooling should not be defined through a notion of leadership that simply sees schools as an adjunct of the corporation. The vision of American education should not be limited to making the United States "number one" in the international marketplace or to more grandiose dreams of presiding over a "new world order". Quite the contrary, the real challenge of leadership is to broaden its definition beyond the ethically truncated parameters of these concerns to the more vital imperatives of educating students to live in a multicultural world, face the challenge of reconciling difference and community, and addressing what it means to have a voice in shaping one's future as part of a broader task of deepening and extending the imperatives of democracy and human rights on both a national and global level. Through such a perspective, leadership takes up the issues of power, culture, and identity within an ethical discourse that points to those practices between the self and others that oblige one "to make an ethical decision, to say: here I stand....here and now I face an other who demands of me an ethical response."[18]

It follows from such a view that leadership poses the issue of responsibility as a social relationship in which difference and otherness becomes articulated into practices which offer resistance to forms of domination and oppression. This raises the need for a discourse on leadership which prompts a discriminating response to others, one which makes students, for example, attentive both to their own implication in particular forms of human suffering and to the oppression of others whose voices demand both recognition and support. Leadership in this view means being able to imagine otherwise, which "entails, at the socio-political level, an 'acting otherwise.'"[19] Richard Kearney has suggested that if educators are not to shrink from the promise of ethical responsibility, they should develop a pedagogical language that emphasizes the importance of being able to identify with others, to empathize with their thoughts and feelings and to develop the capacity for ethical respect. There is also the need to recount the narratives of those others who have become the forgotten victims of history. Through these "absent discourses", teachers and students can narrate "the story of man's (sic) inhumanity to man [and affirm] that the power of human witness can reach beyond silence to others who in remembering the dead are, at the same time, recalled to the moral responsibility of never allowing it to happen again."[20] Finally, educators and others need to develop "the emphatic experience of imaginative practice."[21] This means reconciling the seemingly opposing needs of freedom and solidarity in order to forge a new conception of civic courage and public life.

This suggests a need for educators to redefine the language of leadership in ways that commit administrators, teachers, and students to a discerning conception of democratic community in which the relationship between the self and the other is constituted in practices sustained by historical memories, actualities, and further possibilities of a just and humane society.[22]

Ethically, the crisis of leadership is also evident in the refusal of the new educational reform movement to develop a critical moral discourse. Missing from the current mainstream emphasis on educational reform is a discourse that can illuminate what administrators, teachers, and other cultural workers actually do in terms of the underlying principles and values that structure the stories, visions, and experiences they use to organize and produce particular classroom experiences and social identities. Accountability in current mainstream discourse offers no insights into how schools should prepare students to push against the oppressive boundaries of gender, class, race, and age domination. Nor does such a language provide the conditions for students to interrogate the curriculum as a text deeply implicated in issues and struggles concerning self-identity, culture, power, and history. In effect, the crisis of leadership is grounded, in part, in a refusal to address how particular forms of authority are secured and legitimized at the expense of cultural democracy, critical citizenship, and basic human rights. By refusing to examine the values that not only frame how authority is constructed but also define leadership as a political and pedagogical practice, mainstream educational reformers subordinate the discourse of ethics to the rules of management and efficiency.

Accordingly, leadership in the age of Bush did not focus on how to educate prospective administrators and teachers to address the problems facing public schools in the United States as a crisis of citizenship and ethics. Instead, the infatuation with "leadership" by the Bush Administration and its allies often presupposes that the solution to the problems of American schooling lie in the spheres of management and economics rather than in the realms of values and politics.[23]   It remains to be seen whether or not the Clinton administration is willing to continue with a similar "corporate" approach to school reform.

The Possibilities in Educational Leadership for New Educational Reforms

The new conservative philosophy which permeates mainstream educational reforms is not only suggestive of how to imagine the future, it is also indicative of those "dreams" and "stories" that threaten forms of education integral to the formation of critical citizens capable of exercising civic courage and the moral leadership necessary to promote and advance the language of democracy. It is, furthermore, a signpost indicating one of the major challenges schools of education will have to face. In what follows, I want to address that challenge in somewhat general terms through the construction of what I call the language of demystification and possibility.[24]   I take the word demystification from Cornel West. He argues that "Demystification is a theoretical activity that attempts to give explanations that account for the role and function of specific social practices....demystification gives theory a prominent role and the intellectual a political task....[in highlighting] how modes of interpretation 'serve to sustain social relations which are asymmetrical with regard to the organization of power.'"

Schools of education have a historic opportunity to reclaim the language of substantive democracy, critical citizenship, and social responsibility. Instead of weaving dreams limited to the ever-accelerating demand for tougher tests, accountability schemes, and leadership models forged in the discourse of a sterile technicism, such programs can become part of a collective effort to build and revitalize a democratic culture which is open rather than fixed, disputed rather than given, and supportive rather than intolerant of cultural difference. Leadership programs forged in the twin logic of individual freedom and social justice can attempt to educate existing and future teachers and administrators to work collectively to refuse the role of the disconnected expert and specialist, adopting in its place the role of the engaged and transformative intellectual.

This is not to suggest that administrators, teachers, and students who inhabit schools of education should become wedded to some abstract ideal that removes them from everyday life, that turns them into prophets of perfection and certainty. On the contrary, it suggests a call for schools of education to perform a noble public service: to educate administrators and teachers to undertake social criticism not as outsiders but as public and concerned educators who address the most pressing social and political issues of their neighborhood, community, and society. Rather than celebrating the abstract legacies of expertise and professionalism, leadership, in this case, reconstitutes and rewrites itself through educators who make organic connections with the historical traditions that provide themselves and their students with a voice, history, and sense of belonging.

Schools of education need to inspire their students, by example, to find ways to get involved, to make a difference, and to "lay bare the ways in which meaning is produced and mobilized for the maintenance of relations of domination."[25] This notion of teachers and administrators as engaged intellectuals is not one that simply argues for tolerance. Rather, it is a model of leadership and pedagogical practice marked by forms of political agency and moral courage that expands the meaning of pedagogy to all sites where knowledge and social identities are produced. Such an approach recognizes that education is a process that is not synonymous with the more narrow definition of schooling; it recognizes education as a pedagogical practice that embraces all social and cultural spheres engaged in the production of texts, images, knowledge, values, and identities. In this broader context, the practice of educational leadership serves as a referent for analyzing the relevancies that unite administrators and teachers with other cultural workers who share a similar sense of vocation in combining intellectual work with social responsibility as part of the broader task of "deepening those political [and cultural] practices that go in the direction of a 'radical democracy'."[26] This is form of leadership that links schools to the wider society, one that positions administrators, teachers, students, and others as border intellectuals who constantly move between and across disciplinary, cultural, and social spheres so as to broaden the possibility for dialogue, public conversation, and collective struggle. Peter McLaren calls this approach "an arch of social dreaming."[27]

One starting point for educators to develop an emancipatory theory of leadership might begin with the task of creating a public language that is not only theoretically rigorous, publicly accessible and ethically grounded, but also speaks to a sense of utopian purpose. This language would refuse to reconcile schooling with forms of tracking, testing, and accountability that promote inequality by unconsciously ignoring cultural attributes of disadvantaged racial and class minorities. The vocabulary of educational leadership needs a language which actively acknowledges and challenges those forms of pedagogical silencing which prevent us from becoming aware of and offended by the structures of oppression at work in both institutional and everyday life. Administrators and teachers in schools of education and leadership programs need a new language capable of asking bold questions and generating more critical spaces open to the process of negotiation, translation, and experimentation. At the very least, educators need a language that is interdisciplinary, that moves skillfully among theory, practice, and politics. This is a language that makes the issues of culture, power, and ethics primary to understanding how schools construct knowledge, identities, and ways of life that promote nurturing and empowering relations. We need a language in our leadership programs that defends schools as democratic public spheres responsible for providing an indispensable public service to the nation; a language, in this case, that is capable of awakening the moral, political and civic responsibilities of our youth. More specifically, public schools need to be justified as places in which students are educated in the principles and practices of democracy, but not in a version of democracy cleansed of vision, possibility, or struggle.

Educating for democracy cannot be reduced, as some educators, politicians, and groups have argued, to forcing students to say the pledge of allegiance at the beginning of every school day or to speak and think only in the language of dominant English. Similarly, the most important task facing educators is not about collecting data or the managing of competencies, but the construction of a pedagogical and political vision that recognizes that the problems with American schools lies in the realm of values, ethics, and vision. Put another way, educating for democracy begins not with test scores but with the following questions: "What kinds of citizens do we hope to produce through public education? What kind of society do we want to create?" This involves educating students to live in a critical democracy and suggests a view of empowerment in which learning becomes the basis for challenging social practices that produce symbolic and real violence, that makes some students voiceless and thus powerless, and that also implicates teachers in forms of bigotry, colonialism, and racism. Students need to learn that the relationship between knowledge and power can be emancipatory, that their histories and experiences matter, and that what they say and do can count as part of a wider struggle to change the world around them.

In addition, educators need a language that makes them sensitive to the politics of their own location. At best, such a language would make administrators, teachers, and other cultural workers self-conscious of the historically contingent nature of their own theories, methods, and models of inquiry. As educators, we need to recognize the partiality of our own views in order to render them more suspect and open-ended. We also need to create the conditions and safe-spaces that offer teachers and students the opportunity to be border crossers as part of the effort to learn new languages, refigure the boundaries of interdisciplinary discourse, and to consistently work to make the familiar strange and the given problematic.[28]

The border crossing metaphor is important here because it speaks to the need for reconstructing the language of leadership and reinventing the curricula and pedagogical practices that characterize our programs, schools, and disciplines. This is essentially a question of both what people know and how they come to know it in a particular way within the contexts and constraints of specific social and cultural practices. This suggests some additional considerations.

Administrators and teachers need to work under conditions that allow them to function as intellectuals and not as technicians or clerks. If we are to take the concept of intellectuality seriously as part of a theory and practice of leadership, it means giving educators joint power to shape the conditions under which they work, to produce curriculum that is suited to the interests of the students they actually teach. It also means providing administrators, teachers, and other cultural workers with the time, space, and power necessary during the school day to enable them to work collectively in shaping policy and to work with parents and social service agencies in ways that strengthen school-community ties. Teaching must be linked with empowerment and not merely with technical competence. Teaching is not about carrying out other people's ideas and rules without question. Teaching requires working within conditions in which power is linked to possibility, collective struggle to democratic reforms, and knowledge to the vast terrain of cultural and social differences that map out the terrain of everyday life.

Schools need to close the gap between what they teach and the real world. The curriculum must analyze and deconstruct popular knowledges produced through television and culture industries, and be organized around texts and images that relate directly to the communities, cultures, and traditions that give students a historical sense of identity and place. The content of the curriculum needs to affirm and critically enrich the meaning, language, and knowledge that different students actually use to negotiate and inform their lives. While there is no simple route to incorporating the student experience or popular culture into the curriculum, especially in light of the real fear by students of having these spheres colonized by the schools, it is imperative that these issues be addressed in ways that are as self-critical of the school as they are supportive and critical of the voices and histories that students bring with them to the school.

Public schools need curricula that link the language of the neighborhood, city, and state with the languages of other traditions; a postmodern curricula in which storytelling evokes memories shared and histories made through the affirmation of difference, struggle, and hope. This is not meant to suggest that the experiences that students bring to schools be merely affirmed. On the contrary, one begins with such experiences but does not merely treat them as undisputed or limit what is taught to those experiences. Experience needs to be viewed from a position of empowerment rather than from a position of weakness. Knowledge needs to be made meaningful in order to be made critical and transformative. This suggests that the curriculum be tailored to the voices that students already have so that they can extend those voices into other galaxies, which may be less familiar, but are equally important as terrains of knowledge and possibility.[29]

If administrators and teachers are to take an active role in raising serious questions about what they teach, how they are to teach, and the larger goals for which they are striving, they must take a more critical role in reconstructing a notion of educational leadership that is consistent with what it means to make cultural diversity and social justice central to the notion of pedagogy and democratic life. Hence, educators need to provide new theories that raise issues about how educational leaders can develop an educational project, as Jean-Paul Sartre points out, grounded in a vision of leadership and freedom that embodies a language of both critique and possibility, one that represents both a "flight and a leap ahead, at once refusal and a realization."[30] Teachers need to understand more critically what they know and how they come to know it in a way that enables them to venture into communities of difference in order to reconceptualize the role of the school as both a human service center and a neighborhood resource. This means, as Maxine Greene has been claiming for years, that educational leaders must offer existing and prospective administrators, teachers, and students multiple languages and diverse literacies so that they can communicate across borders of cultural difference, histories, and experiences.[31] The concept of educational leadership is rooted in a notion of multicultural literacy in which social equality and cultural differences co-exist with the principles and practices that inform substantive participatory democracy.[32]

A Language of Critique and Possibility

I want to conclude by emphasizing that prospective and existing educators should be given the opportunity in their schools, in existing teacher education programs, and in conjunction with cultural workers in other pedagogical sites to develop the following elements of a language of critique and possibility.

First, they would be exposed to a language of historical perspective. By perspective I mean the awareness that the way things are is not the way they have always been or must necessarily be in the future. To have perspective is to link the notion of historical inquiry to the imperatives of moral and political agency, it is to locate ourselves and our visions inside of rather than outside of the language of history and possibility. History in this sense does not become something to be discovered, part of the search for an ultimate referent. Instead, it suggests the process of what might be called an imaginative rediscovery. Understood in these terms, history provides multiple referents, codes, voices, and languages and suggests that in the intersection between the past and the present one recognizes a future that offers few guarantees, but is open to dialogue, negotiation, and translation; hence, such a future becomes more accessible and imaginable.

Second, educational administrators, teachers, and students should be immersed in the language of social criticism, rendered here as a deliberate notion of unveiling, negation, and problematizing. This refers to developing the ability and skills to think in oppositional terms, to deconstruct the assumptions and interests that limit and legitimate the very questions we ask as educational leaders. It means understanding the limits of our own language as well as the implications of the social practices we construct on the basis of the language we use to exercise authority and power. It means developing a language that can question public forms, address social injustices, and break the tyranny of the present.

Third, educational leaders need to be skilled in the language of remembrance. Remembrance rejects the notion of knowledge as merely an inheritance with transmission as its only form of practice. Remembrance sees knowledge as a social and historical construction that is always the object of struggle. It is not preoccupied with the ordinary but with what is distinctive and extraordinary. It is concerned not with societies that are quiet, which reduce learning to reverence, procedure and whispers, but with forms of public life that are noisy, that are engaged in dialogue and vociferous speech. In this view, truth is not merely contained in practice, it is also part of the world of recollections, historical memory, and the tales and stories not only of those who have established a well-known legacy of democratic struggle but also those who have too often been silenced, excluded or marginalized.

Fourth, educational leaders need a language of critical imagination, one that both insists on and enables them to consider the structure, movement, and opportunities in the contemporary order of things and how we might act to prevent the barbaric and develop those aspects of public life that point to its best and as yet unrealized possibilities. This is a language of democratic possibilities which asserts that schools play a vital role in developing the political and moral consciousness of its citizens. It is also a grounded in a notion of educational leadership that does not begin with the question of raising test scores, but with a moral and political vision of what it means to educate students to govern, lead a humane life, and address the social welfare of those less fortunate then themselves. This is a notion of leadership that dreams in order to change the world rather than simply manage it.

Finally, educational leaders need to wage a ceaseless campaign to challenge what Daniel Yankelovich has called "the money and missiles sense of reality." This philosophy, Yankelovich explains,

> assumes that what really counts in this world are military power and economic realities, and all the rest is sentimental stuff. It has overly constricted the domain of what is real and transformed the large political and moral dilemmas of our tiem into narrow technical questions that fit the experts' own specialized expertise. This process of technicalizing political issues renders them inaccessible to public understanding and judgment because the public exists in the very domain that is excluded. To narrow issues

artificially is to exclude the bulk of citizenry from the policy-shaping process.33

The money and missile sense of reality needs to be challenged through a different vision of public life, one which demands a reallocation of resources away from the killing machines of the defense industry to programs that insure that every child in this country has the opportunity for gaining access to a free and equal education, and that public schooling be seen as one of the most essential institutions in this country for reconstructing and furthering the imperatives of a democratic and just culture.

Notes

1 For two commentaries on the related nature of the decline of democracy in the United States and the rise of democratic struggles in Eastern Europe and the Soviet Union, see J. Peter Euben, "Democracy in America: Bringing It All Back Home," Bernard Murchland, Ed. *Higher Education and the Practice of Democratic Politics* (Dayton: Kettering Foundation, 1991), pp. 14-22. Henry A. Giroux, *Border Crossings: Cultural Workers and the Politics of Education* (New York: Routledge, 1991), especially chapter 3.

2 J. Peter Euben, "Democracy in America," op. cit., p. 17.

3 Richard Kearney, "Ethics and the Postmodern Imagination," *Thought* 62:244 (March 1987), p.51.

4 For a revealing analysis of some of these issues, see Kevin Phillips, *The Politics of the Rich and the Poor* (New York: Harper Perennial, 1991). For an analysis of how these issues relate to education, see Svi Shapiro, *Between Capitalism and Democracy* (New York: Bergin and Garvey, 1990); *Democracy: A Group Project* (Seattle: Bay Press, 1990). Henry A. Giroux, *Schooling and the Struggle for Public Life*, (Minneapolis: University of Minnesota Press, 1988); Maxine Greene, *The Dialectic of Freedom* (New York: Teachers College Press, 1988); Peter McLaren, *Life in Schools* (New York: Longman, Inc., 1989).

5 This issue is taken up in Nancy Fraser, *Unruly Practices: Power, Discourse and Gender in Contemporary Social Theory* (Minneapolis: University of Minnesota Press, 1989); Stuart Hall and David Held, "Citizens and Citizenship," Stuart Hall and Martin Jacques, Eds. *New Times: The Changing Face of Politics in the 1990s* (London: Verso, 1989), pp. 173-188; Henry A. Giroux, *Schooling and the Struggle for Public Life* (Minneapolis: University of Minnesota Press, 1988).

6 Joan Lipsitz, "Scenes from the New American Civil War," Samuel Halperin,Ed. *Voices from the Field* (Washington, D. C. William T. Grant Foundation Commission on Work, Family and Citizenship and the Institute for Educational Leadership, 1991), p. 37.

7 For programs that work, see Henry M. Levin, *Accelerated Schools for At-Risk Students*, CPRE Research Report Series RR-010 (New Brunswick, N.J.: Center for Policy Research in Education, Rutgers University, 1988); Henry M. Levin, "At-Risk Students in a Yuppie Age," *Educational Policy* Vol. 4, no. 4 (1990), pp. 283-295; Daniel Schorr, *Within Our Reach: Breaking the Cycle of Disadvantage* (New York: Doubleday, 1987); Deborah Meier, "Central Park East: An Alternative Story," *Phi*

Delta Kappan (June 1987), pp. 753-757; James Comer, *School Power* (New York: Free Press, 1980).

[8] For an analysis of existing conditions of poverty, see *Child Poverty in America* (Washington, D.C.: Children's Defense Fund, 1991); see also, *Beyond Rhetoric: A New American Agenda for Children and Families: Final Report* (Washington, D. C.: National Commission on Children, 1991); Jonathan Kozol, *Savage Inequalities: Children in America's Schools* (New York: Crown Publishers, 1991).

[9] For an excellent analysis of how the politics of not naming works in public schools, see Michelle Fine, *Framing Dropouts: Notes on the Politics of an Urban Public School* (Albany, SUNY Press, 1991), especially chapter 2.

[10] Deborah Meier, "Bush and the Schools: A Hard Look," *Dissent* (Summer 1991), p. 329. Choice does not have to be defined in terms that reduce it to either the issue of vouchers or the imperatives of the market. For some interesting comments on the history, meaning, and struggle over choice as part of the language of democratic empowerment, see Jo Nathan "Results and the Future Prospects of State efforts to Increase Choice Among Schools," *Phi Delta Kappan*, (June 1987), pp. 749-752; Mary Anne Raywid, "Public Choice, Yes; Vouchers, No!" *Phi Delta Kappan*, (June 1987), pp. 762-769; Deborah Meier, "Choice Can Save Public Education," *The Nation*, (March 4, 1991), pp. 253, 266-271; Henry A. Giroux and Peter McLaren," *America 2000* and the Politics of Erasure: Democracy and Cultural Difference Under Siege," *International Journal of Educational Reform* (forthcoming).

11 Stuart Hall, " And Not A Shot Fired," *Marxism Today* (December 1991), p.13.

[12] Needless to say, Chubb and Moe's *Politics, Markets, and American Schools* is the subject of heated debate, which in some cases creates strange bedfellows from among the radicals and neo-conservatives, see for example: Herbert Gintis, Baroness Cox, Anthony Green, and Mike Hickox, "Politics, Markets, and America's Schools", *British Journal of Sociology of Education* Vol. 12, no. 3 (1991), pp. 381-396; for an excellent analysis of the elitist and conservative assumptions that inform Chubb and Moe's book, see Francis C. Fowler, "The Shocking Ideological Integrity of Chubb and Moe," *Journal of Education* (forthcoming); for a superb alternative perspective on educational reform, see Terry A. Astuto and David Clark L. Clark, "Challenging the Limits of School Restructuring and Reform," (*NSSE Yearbook*, forthcoming).

[13] Chantal Mouffe, "The Civics Lesson," *New Statesman and Society* (October 7, 1988), p. 29.

[14] Robert Bellah, et.al., "Breaking the Tyranny of the Market," *Tikkun* 6:4 (1991), pp. 30-32, 89-91.

15 Robert Bellah, et.al., *Habits of the Heart* (Berkeley, Ca.: University of California Press, 1985), p. 23.

16 Bellah, et. al., Ibid. p. 90.

17 This issue is taken up in Roger I. Simon, Don Dippo, and Arleen Schenke, *Learning Work: A Critical Pedagogy of Work Education* (New York: Bergin and Garvey, 1991).

18 Richard Kearney, *The Wake of Imagination* (Minneapolis: University of Minnesota Press, 1988), p. 361.

19 Ibid., p. 457.

20 Richard Kearney, *Poetics of Imagining: From Husserl to Lyotard* (New York: Harper Collins, 1991), p. 223.

21 Kearney, Ibid., p. 226.

22 Of course, the issue of emancipatory leadership has been taken up by others, though this discourse is marginal to the larger field of educational administration. For example, see William Foster, *Paradigms and Promises: New Approaches to Educational Administration* (Buffalo: Prometheus, 1986); Richard A. Quantz, Nelda Cambron-McCabe, and Michael Dantley, "Preparing School Administrators for Democratic Authority: A Critical Approach to Graduate Education," *The Urban Review* 23:1 (1991), pp. 3-19; Spencer J. Maxcy, *Educational Leadership: A Critical Pragmatic Perspective* (New York: Bergin and Garvey, 1991).

23 The reduction of democracy to issues of management and social engineering can be seen clearly in both the business community and academic community. Edward Bernays, the alleged founder of the science of public relations described the "engineering of consent" as the "essence of democracy." Bernays clearly understood that the people who have the resources and power also have the means to reduce democracy to a marketing campaign. Given that Bernays made this comment in the 1920s, he may be one of the original theoreticians of the postmodern age where the image or simulacrum replace reality and the politics of representation replaces the politics of everyday life. Of course, the potential of democracy has also been expressed as part of a politics of containment in which real democratic participation was derided as an "excess of democracy." For example, see Michael Crozier, Samuel P. Huntington, and Joji Watanuke, *The Crisis of Democracy* (New York: New York University Press, 1975). For an interesting analysis of these issues, see Noam Chomsky, *Necessary Illusions: Thought Control in Democratic Societies* (Boston: South End Press, 1989); Noam Chomsky, "Media Control: The Spectacular Achievements of Propaganda" (Westfield, NJ: *Open Magazine*, 1991).

24 In Cornel West, "Decentering Europe," *Critical Inquiry* 33:1 (1991), pp. 22-23.

25 Cornel West, "Theory, Pragmatism, and Politics," Jonathan Arac and Barbara Johnson, Eds. *Consequences of Theory* (Baltimore: The Johns Hopkins University Press, 1991), p. 22.

26 *Strategies* Collective, "Building a New Left: An Interview with Ernesto Laclau," *Strategies*, No. 1 (Fall 1988), p. 23. See also a special issue of *New Formations*, Number 14 (Summer 1991), which is entirely devoted to the theme, "On Democracy." See also, Robert A. Dahl, *Democracy and its Critics* (New Haven: Yale University Press, 1989).

27 Peter McLaren, "Schooling and the Postmodern Body: Critical Pedagogy and the Politics of Enfleshment," in Henry A. Giroux, *Postmodernism, Feminism, and Cultural Politics* (Albany: SUNY Press, 1991), p. 170.

28 This issue is brilliantly developed in the works of many postcolonial theorists who provide an invaluable source of insight for educational theorists. On the politics of location issue, see James Clifford, *The Predicament of Culture* (Cambridge: Harvard University Press, 1988), especially chapter 4 on ethnographic surrealism. Also see, Robert Young, *White Mythologies: Writing History and the West* New York: Routledge, 1990); Stanley Aronowitz and Henry A. Giroux, *Postmodern Education: Politics, Culture, and Social Criticism* (Minneapolis: University of Minnesota Press, 1991); Peter McLaren, Ed. *Postmodernism, Postcolonialism, and Pedagogy* (Victoria, Australia: James Nicholas Publishers, 1991).

29 Henry A. Giroux, *Schooling and the Struggle for Public Life* (Minneapolis: University of Minnesota Press, 1988); bell hooks, *Talking Back* (Boston: South End Press, 1989). On the issue of everyday life, popular culture, and schooling, see Henry A. Giroux, Roger I. Simon, and Contributors, *Popular Culture, Schooling, and Everyday Life* (New York: Bergin and Garvey, 1989).

30 Jean-Paul Sartre, *Search for a Method* (New York: Alfred A. Knopf, 1963), p. 92.

31 For example, see: Maxine Greene, *The Dialectic of Freedom* (New York: Teachers College Press, 1988).

32 Nancy Fraser, *Unruly Practices* (Minneapolis: University of Minnesota Press, 1989.

33. Daniel Yankelovich, "How the Public Learns the Public's Business," *Kettering Review* (Winter, 1985), p.11.

2.

Reclaiming the Social

Pedagogy, Resistance, and Politics in Celluloid Culture

We live in an age in which the new conservativism that has reigned in the United States for the last decade has consistently struggled to depoliticize politics while simultaneously attempting to politicize popular culture and the institutions that make up daily life. The depoliticizing of politics is evident, in part, in the ways in which the new conservative formations use the electronic technologies of image, sound, and text not only to alter traditional systems of time, space, and history, but also to displace serious political issues to the realm of the aesthetic and the personal.[1] In this context, discourses of style, form, and authenticity are employed to replace questions concerning how power is mobilized by diverse dominant groups to oppress, marginalize, and exploit large portions of the American population. Understood in ideological terms, the depoliticizing of politics is about the attempt to construct citizens who believe that they have little or no control over their lives and that issues of identity, culture, and agency bear no relationship to or "acknowledgment of mediations: material, historical, social, psychological, and ideological" (Solomon-Godeau xxviii). Hence, the depoliticizing of the political represents a complex, though incomplete, effort by the new conservatism to secure a politics of representation that attempts to render the workings of its own ideology indiscernible. That is, dominant groups seize upon the dynamics of cultural power to secure their own interests while simultaneously attempting to make the political context and ideological sources of such power invisible.

In the current historical conjuncture there is an ongoing attempt by the forces of the new right to replace the practice of substantive democracy with a democracy of images. At the same time, the discourse of responsible citizenship is subordinated to the marketplace imperatives of choice, consumption, and standardization. This is particularly true with respect to public schools. The Reagan/Bush Administrations drastically cut financial support for public school programs, systematically attempted to reprivatize the public school sector by sponsoring legislation that would allow public money to be used to support private schooling, and linked educational reforms to the needs of big business.[2]   Moreover, the new conservatives have made schooling an intense site of struggle in their efforts to eliminate non-canonical and subordinate cultures as serious objects of knowledge.[3]

The struggle over the economic and political apparatuses of the state has largely been extended principally by new conservative formations to the sphere of culture.[4] Contrary to the conventional left thinking, as Laclau and Mouffe have pointed out, the greatest challenge to the right and its power may be lodged not in the mobilization of universal agents such as the working class or some other oppressed group, but in a cultural struggle in which almost every facet of daily life takes on a degree of undecidability and thus becomes unsettled and open to broader collective dialogue and multiple struggles.

What has become important to recognize is that the new conservative bloc, while firmly controlling the state and its major apparatuses, turned its attention during the Reagan/Bush era towards the wider terrain of culture and identified higher education, public schooling, the art world, and rock music as visible targets.[5] This is evident in the right wing blitz organized around issues such as pornography, political correctness, and multiculturalism and testifies to a new level of hegemonic struggle over the institutions and discourses through which a politics of representation is directly linked to the production of mobile fields of knowledge, shifting and multiple social identities, and new cultural formations. The war being waged by the new conservative bloc is not simply over profit or the securing of traditional forms of authority, it is over the emergence of decentered and diverse oppositional discourses, such as feminism, postmodernism, and postcolonialism, that have begun to call into question all of the grand narratives of modernism with its unfettered conviction in science and technology as the engine of progress, its unflinching belief in the humanist subject as the unified agent of history, and its adamant insistence that Western culture is synonymous with the very notion of civilization itself. What is interesting regarding these struggles is that they not only pose an emerging threat to the dominant order, but they also offer a new set of discourses and strategies that are being taken very seriously by the new right. The dominant conservative formations in the United States appear haunted and besieged by the emergence of the discourses and cultures of difference that refuse to remain silent or confined to the margins of history, power, and politics. This new politics of cultural difference has important implications for redefining the notions of hegemony, resistance, and struggles over forms of self and social representation.[6]

Within the paradox of the reality of depoliticization, the politicization of culture, and the emerging politics of difference, hegemony has to be read as always fractured, contradictory, and decentered. Moreover, domination does not present itself as a universal practice, exhausting those it oppresses. In actuality, hegemonic power can only be understood in its specificity, in its constant attempt to restructure and refigure its strengths and weaknesses, and in its continual attempt to recuperate forms of resistance that are as ongoing as they are different. I believe that new opportunities present themselves for deepening the pedagogical as a form of cultural politics in what Jim Collins has identified as the decentered power struggles that constitute both hegemonic and counter-hegemonic movements.

In what follows, I want to examine how the pedagogical can be taken up as a form of cultural production that reworks the relationship between cultural texts, teachers, and students. On the one hand, this means developing a theoretical case for using popular cultural texts such as film, television, advertisements, music videos, and mass circulation magazines as serious objects of knowledge related to the power of self-definition and the struggle for social justice. Equally important is the necessary refusal to take up popular culture within a liberal pedagogical model that reduces its use to a discourse of relevance or the narrow, methodological imperative to teach the conflicts.[7]   On the other hand, I want to reassert the importance of critical pedagogy as a form of cultural practice which does not simply tell the student how to think or what to believe, but provides the conditions for a set of ideological and social relations which engender diverse possibilities for students to produce rather than simply acquire knowledge, to be self-critical about both the positions they describe and the locations from which they speak, and to make explicit the values that inform their relations with others as part of a broader attempt to produce the conditions necessary for either the existing society or a new and more democratic social order.[8]

As part of examining the relationship between popular culture and critical pedagogy, I want to avoid using a binary framework that locates schooling in a context which focuses either on how schools monolithically reproduce the dominant social order through particular forms of social and cultural reproduction or how students contest the dominant society through various forms of resistance. Instead, I want to analyze radical pedagogy as a theoretical discourse that helps to illuminate how cultural texts can be understood as part of a complex and often contradictory set of ideological and material processes through which the transformation of knowledge, identities, and values takes place. Such texts, like schools in this sense, produce narratives, desires, and subjectivities that are far from homogeneous and in turn encounter students whose own subjectivities are constructed in multiple, complex, and contradictory ways.

Central to such a task are at least three important issues. First, there is the task of redefining teachers as cultural workers, that is, as educators committed to a political project and normatively based discourse that expands the possibility for radical democracy. Second, there is the issue of reclaiming popular culture as a complex terrain of pedagogical struggle without romanticizing it. Third, pedagogy must be viewed as the deliberate attempt to produce knowledge, forms of ethical address, and social identities.[9] More specifically, a pedagogy of the popular would take as its objective the interrogation of traditional positivist and modernist notions of the curriculum and canonicity, the rupturing of the universalized view of identity as a privatized consciousness, and the elimination of the view that cultural difference is a threat to civic democratic culture. I will attempt to take up some of these issues by analyzing a class I taught on education and the politics of identity, focusing primarily on the use of the film, *Dead Poets Society*.

Popular cultural texts such as *Dead Poets Society* should be analyzed within the discourse of political economy and transnational capitalism, within social reading formations that inscribe such texts with overdetermined meanings, one being that their function is to entertain rather than signify; they must be analyzed as commodities that implicate even as they are taken up in order to subvert the very system that produces them. But most importantly for my purposes, films such as *Dead Poets Society* are neither the bearers of monolithic themes, nor should they be read simply as sites of conflicting ideologies. On the contrary, rather than reducing such a text to the reified terrain of relevance and teaching the conflicts, it should be posited as a site of struggle over how representations mean differently and what the consequences of such differences might be if they are to matter as part of a wider theoretical, ethical, and political discourse. Secondly, *Dead Poets Society* can be engaged not only to deconstruct how it represents a particular view of the political, but also how it functions to secure specific forms of affective investments. What is it in films such as *Dead Poets Society*, for instance, that mobilizes specific desires, identifications, and needs? And finally, how might students engage this film critically as part of a broader discourse of ethics and politics that promotes a deeper understanding of the historical and cultural locations from which they might speak, act, and struggle?

Pedagogy, Resistance, and Celluloid Culture

During the Fall of 1991, I taught an undergraduate class for teachers in training on curriculum and secondary education. The class consisted of mostly white, middle and upper middle class students. Most of the work we had been analyzing in the class consisted largely of exposing the role that schools play in the process of social and cultural reproduction. I wanted to go beyond this type of analysis by introducing students to films and other texts in which both teachers and students exhibited forms of resistance in the classroom. One assignment consisted of having the students choose a popular cultural form which addressed the issue of pedagogy and schooling. At issue here was having the students analyze the relationship between their own experiences in schools and those portrayed in popular cultural forms. The class largely decided to focus on Hollywood films, and finally choose to view two films, *Dead Poets Society* and *Stand and Deliver*.

In one sense, *Dead Poets Society* was an exemplary film to use pedagogically because it had been suggested by some students as a text which embodied much of what was perceived as the political and pedagogical principles encouraged in the course. That is, the film was comprehended as "living out" the perceived requirements and practices of critical teaching. What became apparent to me was that my students' initial motivations in choosing the film had less to do with an analytical reading of the text than it did with an investment in the film that was largely affective. According to my students, *Dead Poets Society* was valuable as an exemplary model of critical pedagogy because it staked out a terrain of hope, and offered subject positions from within which they could project an image of themselves as future teachers; an image that encouraged them to identify themselves as agents rather than as mere technicians. As some students pointed out, the film made them feel good about themselves as teachers-in-the-making.

In my view, the film presented a model of liberal pedagogy, in part, by mobilizing popular sentiment through what Larry Grossberg has called an "affective epidemic." That is, even though the film takes as its central narrative the issue of resistance, its structure undermined a critical reading of its own codes by establishing a strong emotional affinity between the viewers and the progressive teacher portrayed in this film.

The pedagogical challenge presented by *Dead Poets Society* was grounded in making clear the multiple and often contradictory ways in which it ruptured and supported dominant codes regarding issues of knowledge, pedagogy, and resistance. Deconstructing this film was not meant as a pedagogical exercise in canceling the affective and meaning-making investments students brought to it. Nor was my pedagogical approach meant as an attempt to provide a definitive ideological reading of the film. On the contrary, I wanted to address how the mobilization of meaning and affective investments within the film's form and content functioned as part of a broader cultural and pedagogical practice that was neither innocent nor politically neutral. What has to be recognized here is a central dilemma faced by educators who engage the popular as part of a broader pedagogical project. The dilemma is constituted by the need to challenge the structures of meaning and affect without delegitimating the importance of the varied investments mobilized within the students' response to the film. Hence, I wanted to take up the film as a cultural form which produced knowledge in the service of particular forms of authority, proffered conditions for agency which privileged some groups over others, and revealed contradictory and partial insights regarding how oppression works through various aspects of schooling.

Canonicity, Pedagogy, and Resistance in "Dead Poets Society"

Dead Poets Society (1989), directed by Peter Weir and written by Tom Schulman, is set in a boys boarding school, Welton Academy. The opening shots of the film portray Welton Academy as an exclusive prep school, situated in a picture postcard setting that tries hard to emulate the beauty and peacefulness of the English countryside. The school itself has all the aesthetic trappings of an Ivy League college. The architecture of the school is monumentalist and Gothic. The students, teachers, and parents are from the ruling class. The parents and students move easily within a cultural capital that signifies privilege, wealth, and power. Social identities in this film are constructed within an unspoken yet legitimating discourse that privileges whiteness, patriarchy, and heterosexuality as the universalizing norms of identity. Precisely because it exists outside of the context of racial difference, whiteness as a basis of privilege in *Dead Poets Society* becomes "invisible" because there is no context to render it visible as a dominant racial category, as a mark of power and identity that refuses to call attention to itself.[10] Set in 1959, the "whiteness" of the faculty and students is an historically accurate representation; however, *Dead Poets Society* suspends the dynamics of historical contingency and specificity within a reactionary nostalgia. An aura of universality radiates through this film which expresses its cultural and political narratives within a mythical, timeless age when the messy relations of democracy, cultural difference, and social struggle were kept in place, or at least out of sight; when aesthetics took precedence over politics, and students (of privilege) were safely cushioned within monastic borders removed from the potentially antagonistic relations of everyday life. The politics and aesthetics of nostalgia in this film mobilize affective identifications and investments in order to secure the authority of a particular history, "that story which institutionally seeks to legitimate a continuum of sense, which as [Walter] Benjamin insisted, has to be blasted apart" (Chambers, 78).

In the opening address to the parents and students of Welton, the headmaster celebrates Welton's record of academic achievement, pointing out that over 75 percent of its graduates go on to attend Ivy League schools. There is no pretense here. Welton is less concerned about teaching its students how to think than it is in preparing them to assume positions of power. Within this context, pedagogy defines itself through a ruthless instrumentalism removed from the progressive goals of creating the conditions for critical agency, ethical accountability, and the obligations of democratic public life. As the film shifts to portray the dynamics of classroom life, it becomes clear that the curriculum is a no frills version of high-culture canonicity, and the pedagogy used by the all white, male teachers emphasizes a numbing combination of discipline and transmission as the prevailing pedagogical practices.

Initially, the students appear to fully embrace this anesthetized reactionary environment. For instance, on the first day of school they trade stories about having gone to summer school in order to get the edge over their classmates; the routinization and authoritarianism of the school appears to shape every aspect of their lives unproblematically; they appear to be academic zombies living out the projections and wishes of their successful fathers. Moreover, every other older male figure at this school who figures prominently as a surrogate father reinforces the same unproblematic relation to the competitive milieu. It's hardly surprising then, that before the semester classes even begin a number of boys decides to form a study group that will meet that very evening.

An unsettling of sorts occurs with the appearance at Welton of a new English teacher named Mr. Keating, played by Robin Williams. Framed against the deadening pedagogy of his peers, Keating appears to be witty, unconventional, and courageous. In his first meetings with the class, he ruptures traditional pedagogical standards by having them rip out the introduction to their poetry book, which equates reading poetry to the same logic one would use to measure the heights of trees. This is not merely deconstruction, this is a textual assault that attempts to relocate poetry within the interests and voices the students actually bring to the class. Keating doesn't simply want them to read poetry, he wants them to undertake it as a form of cultural production. According to him, poetry is about the relationship between passion and beauty. He tell his students "The powerful play goes on and you may contribute a verse." For Keating, poetry offers the basis not for social empowerment but self empowerment. Keating wants to resurrect the humanist subject within an aesthetic of resistance, and eschews any notion of resistance which calls into question how the operations of power work to promote human suffering, and social injustice, and exploitation. Keating's invocation to his students "Carpe diem, lads! Seize the day! Make your lives extraordinary" is expressed in forms of pedagogical resistance that celebrate the privatized ego of ruling class boys without any reference or analysis of how dominant social forms work subjectively to make these students complicit with the hierarchies of domination that inform the organization of the school, the curriculum, and the social formations that influence a wider society, to which Keating never alludes.

Resistance in Keating's pedagogy suggests a strangely empty quality. He has students stand on their desks so they can see the world from another position. Looking at the room from the top of their desks has an ironic twist to it since most of these students will be looking at the world when they leave school from the pinnacle of power rather than from the horizontal spaces that most people occupy at the bottom of the social and economic pyramid. On another occasion, Keating takes his students to the school courtyard and asks them to march in different strides. The pedagogical lesson taught in this case is that they must learn how to swim against the stream, to find "their own walk." In one celebrated scene in the film, Keating makes a particularly shy student get up before the class, asks him to close his eyes and free associate on a phrase from Whitman, "I sound my barbaric Yawp over the roofs of the world." The boy stutters, Keating whirls the student around and encourages him to speak to the metaphor. The boy finally attempts to articulate a poem and his classmates respond with resounding applause. In this instance, the audience is positioned to see Keating as a sensitive, caring teacher, who creates a space for the student that is metaphorically safe for the student and the audience.

In *Dead Poets Society*, resistance demands no sacrifices, no risks, no attempt to deconstruct the relationship between the margins and the centers of power. On the contrary, resistance in Keating's pedagogy serves to depoliticize and decontextualize since it is only developed within a romanticized aesthetic. In fact, even Keating doesn't appear to understand how he is complicitous with dominant relations of power. If he does possess such recognition, it is likely couched in a conventional bourgeois resignation guided by the conviction that poverty and suffering will always be with us; in fact, they may even be good for the soul. He appears to represent the classic modernist teacher whose pedagogical sensibilities have been spawned by Enlightenment thinking, with its narratives of unending progress, faith in a unified social world, and the power of an unencumbered individualism. Keating wants to be loved but is incapable of recognizing that resistance is less the production of a vapid and aesthetic individualism rooted in the traditions of British high culture than it is a call for solidarity and collective action. This is largely due to the aesthetics surrounding his epistemology, his particular "style" of coming to know something that obscures deeper political and social issues. In fact, as soon as Keating's unorthodox teaching methods appear to threaten the legitimating ideology of the school, he resorts to the discourse of accommodation rather than resistance. For example, when Keating is blamed for the suicide of one of his students, he refuses to challenge the trumped-up charges on the part of the headmaster, Mr. Knowland, and accepts his fate passively by simply leaving the school. As soon as politics crosses over into the realm of power and politics, Keating resents himself as incapable of acting on his own behalf. His pedagogical call to make one's life extraordinary reveals itself as rhetoric that limits rather than expands the capacity for human agency and struggle. There is nothing extraordinary in Keating's failure to resist at the end of this film.

Another major subtext of the film centers around the influence that Keating has on a group of students in his English class who discover that, as a former student of Welton Academy, Keating founded the Dead Poets Society. The students immediately query Keating about the society and what it meant and are told that Keating and a group of friends found a cave off campus and read the poetry of the Romantics in order to "suck the marrow out of life [while] letting poetry drip from our tongue." With the sensitive Neil Perry as their leader, a group of Keating's admirers proceed to recuperate the Dead Poets Society. It is here that the boys begin their own journey of resistance. They violate school rules by meeting in a cave off campus. Initially, they meet to read the Romantic poets, they then resort to reading their own poetry, smoking, playing musical instruments while emulating beat poetry, and bringing some girls to the cave. In one of the final cave scenes, a member of the group proclaims that he wants to be called Nuwanda, and in a striking display of colonialism takes on the identity of the Other as the province of the primitive, exotic, and romanticized warrior. Other acts of resistance that inform the boys' behavior unfold when Neil Perry defies the wishes of a particularly stern father to concentrate on his course work by taking a role in a local play; another student, Knox Overstreet, boldly pursues a public high school cheerleader at the risk of being beaten up by her boyfriend; and Charlie Dalton puts a notice in the school newspaper signed by the Dead Poets Society calling for the admission of women to Welton Academy.

The dynamics of power and student resistance collide around two issues. In the first instance, Dalton is berated and paddled by Mr. Knowland, the headmaster, for standing up at a school assembly and mocking him by announcing that the headmaster has a call from God. Dalton, who is from a wealthy family, takes his punishment but refuses to give the headmaster the names of other members of the Dead Poets Society. Neil Perry, a pivotal character in the film, is torn between the individualism encouraged by Keating and the tyrannical demands imposed on him by his father. Finally, when his father discovers him acting in the school play, he pulls Neil out of Welton and threatens to send him off to a military school the next day. Neil leaves Welton and shortly afterwards commits suicide. There is a curious twist here. Neil Perry comes from a family that is lower middle class; his father constantly justifies his own imperious manner by arguing that he wants Neil to have the education and social status he never had the chance to experience. Neil in this context becomes the Other, the class-specific misfit who lacks the wealth and privilege to take risks, to move easily within the demands and imperatives of ruling class culture. The message of *Dead Poets Society* seems clear in this case. Resistance for members of this class of "climbers" is not only out of place, it ultimately leads to self-destruction. On the other hand, Charlie Dalton challenges the authority of the headmaster, gets expelled from Welton, and yet there is no doubt because of his wealth and family position that his life will not be altered drastically. He belongs to the culture of the winners, resistance is simply harmless play, in which one can afford to engage when one moves in circles of privilege. In this context, risk translates into an aesthetic, an inconvenience or maybe an interesting story to be repeated later by an adult recalling his own resistance as simply part of a rite of passage engaged in within the hallowed traditions of an oppressive but pragmatic form of schooling.

As played out in *Dead Poets Society*, resistance is more often than not an emotional breach of convention and received social realities; it has more to do with a particular change in personal disposition towards an event than changing the structural conditions of events themselves. Resistance here is used as a form of cultural negotiation rather than social transformation.[11]

Following Neil Perry's suicide, the headmaster in an attempt ward off any negative publicity for the school uses Keating as a scapegoat. In the investigation that follows, the group of boys who idolize Keating are obliged to sign statements indicating that he forced them into resurrecting the Dead Poets Society, filled their heads with heretical thoughts, and was directly responsible for Neil's decision to appear in the school play, disobey his father, and thus commit suicide. With the exception of one member of the group all of the boys sign the statement, rat on their teacher, and continue with their lives at Welton as if nothing had happened. In the final scene of the film, Keating comes back to his office to collect his personal belongings. He has to pass through his English class which is now being taught by Knowland, the headmaster. As he is about to exit, some of the boys in the class as a gesture of nonconformity stand up on their respective desks as a show of support for Keating. He smiles at them and says "thank you boys." Hence, in the end, resistance, betrayal, and repressive authority are reworked and reconciled in a discourse of politeness which cancels out dominating relations of power and those who are complicitous with it. Keating remains the well-mannered man until the end, confirming the idea that resistance does not permanently change the world but merely interrupts it only to return us to the canonical past in which tradition, patriarchy, and Eurocentricism continue to provide a sense of order and continuity. The relationship between power and knowledge in Keating's pedagogy of resistance betrays itself by claiming that the alternative to stuffy textbooks is British and American Romanticism of the 19th Century, not the socially engaged literature of the day.[12]

One of the most pernicious subtexts in the film is organized around the construction of gendered subject positions in which women are represented in terms that are misogynist and demeaning.[13]

Understood in these terms, *Dead Poets Society* does more than ignore structured inequalities in the wider society, depoliticize resistance, and naturalize how the canon is used to produce racist and class-specific practices. It also legitimates gendered social practices through various images and representations in which sexual identity is inscribed in various forms of sexist domination. This is most obviously evidenced in the relegation of women in this film to either trophies or appendages of male power. In one glaring example, Keating tells the "boys" that one of the central purposes of poetry is to "woo women." In this case, resistance as a form of "hip" pedagogical posturing is structured through the legitimation of sexist social relations. This lesson is certainly not lost on Keating's boys. While meeting in the cave, one of the boys reads a poem that is written on the back of a *Playboy* centerfold. Resistance for Keating's boys appears to support rather than rupture their own patriarchal identities. On another occasion, the girls who are brought to the cave are treated as if they are too dumb to recognize or understand the poetry of the Romantics. Following a similar logic, Knox's courtship with the public school cheerleader serves to reduce her to a reified object of desire and pleasure. Even the call by Keating's "resisters" to admit girls to Welton Academy transparently reveals itself as an opportunity for the boys to get more dates, to offset their academic work with sexual pleasure. In the end, resistance, knowledge, and pedagogy come together in *Dead Poets Society* to harness identity and power to the misogynist interests and fortunes of patriarchy. Within this coming-of-age narrative, whiteness reasserts itself through the logic of cultural racism, class discrimination, and the objectification of women. This is not merely a foreshortened view of gender relations within prep school culture, it is an active assertion, a politics of representation, in which resistance is incorporated as a pedagogical practice that actively produces sexism as part of its own legacy of power and domination.

Pedagogical Authority and the Politics of the Popular

In order to structure a position from which students might understand how their own subject positions are partly constructed within a dominant Eurocentric assemblage of liberal humanism mobilized within configurations of meaning and desire, I used the presentation of *Dead Poets Society* to raise important questions about the ideological interests at work in forms of textual authority that foster particular reading practices. In taking up this issue, I framed my discussion of the film with my students around a number of important pedagogical concerns. These included: How are readers' choices defined and limited by the range of readings made available through the representations mobilized by particular forms of textual authority? How do power and authority articulate between the wider society and the classroom so as to create the conditions at work in constructing particular discourses in the reading of this film? The tension I had to confront was how to address the power of hope and agency provided by the discourse of liberal humanism without destroying a sense of pedagogical possibility.

For me, the pedagogical challenge presented itself in trying to engage the film as a mode of writing, which took the form of allowing the students to make the "texts" mean differently by reorganizing the systems of intertextual, ideological, and cultural references in which it was constructed historically and semiotically, and in relation to wider social events. In the first instance, this meant giving students the opportunity to analyze the plurality of meanings that informed the film. This was done by having students view the film from the perspective of their own experiences and histories by writing short, critical papers, which they then duplicated and shared with the rest of the class for dialogue and comment. It was at this point that the students' initial affective investments in the film were mediated critically by other texts presented to the class, and dialogically voiced and challenged. As well, I introduced magazine and newspaper reviews along with my own written commentary on the film. The pedagogical issue here centered on both having the teacher's voice heard, but at the same time providing the conditions for such a voice to be engaged and challenged. Roger Simon has referred to this pedagogical moment as the reaffirmation of both critical authority and the struggle over the sign. He notes that such a struggle has to be ongoing because, if it stops, learning itself stops.

Once students analyzed how the film can be read differently to mobilize different forms of affect and meaning, diverse points of identification, they were given the opportunity to analyze how *Dead Poets Society* might be understood within the larger framework that informed the course. This suggested analyzing how the film mobilized particular, if not contradictory, relations of domination and possibility, and how such relations articulate with some of the conservative educational reform policies advocated by the past Bush Administration. Within this frame, a number of students addressed how *Dead Poets Society* could be understood within some of the current problems regarding issues of race, class and gender. For instance, students discussed how the film might be taught as part of an anti-racist pedagogy and how the film both excludes cultural differences and erases whiteness as a privileged racial category. The class also discussed how this film reproduced patriarchal relations and how it might be read from a variety of feminist discourses. Of course, there were students whose positions did not change, and who actively argued from a liberal humanist discourse. These students were able to affirm and defend their positions, without being subjected to a form of pedagogical terrorism which would put their identities on trial.

Finally, the class took up the related issues of identity, class, and cultural differences by watching *Stand and Deliver* (directed by Roman Menendez), which portrays a math teacher, Jamie Escalante (Edward James Olmos) similarly engaged in an act of resistance. Here, however, the setting is a contemporary public school in the barrio in East Los Angeles. Fighting the lethal conditions of overcrowding, lack of resources, and institutional inertia (read as racism), Escalante wages a one-man war against the system in order to "save the barrio kids." Escalante combines a form of pedagogical wizardry and authoritarianism in challenging both the students and the school. He speaks to his students in both Spanish and English, and he affirms their cultural capital while extending their expectations of success and possibility. Inspiring them to reach beyond the inequities and discrimination that routinely structure their daily school experiences and aspirations, he introduces them to the alien world of calculus, which signifies high academic status and is the mark of a privileged cultural currency in the school curriculum. As the film unfolds, Escalante's notion of resistance translates into getting the students to study hard, pass the Advanced Placement Test in calculus, and hopefully get a chance to go on to college.

I think *Stand and Deliver* is ultimately a very conservative film. That is, it appropriates elements of a progressive pedagogy to affirm the problematic goal of teaching for the test and legitimizing canonical knowledge rather than getting "students to think critically about their place in relation to the knowledge they gain and to transform their world view fundamentally by taking the politics of knowledge seriously" (Mohanty, 192). On the other hand, *Stand and Deliver* does spark serious questions about racial discrimination, the specificity of the cultural context of teaching, and the importance of teachers and students engaging in the process of negotiation and translation in order to engage both beyond it as part of a broader attempt at self and social empowerment. But like *Dead Poets Society*, the film does not link resistance to recognizing the "materiality of conflict, of privilege, and of domination" (Mohanty, 206). Resistance in both films provides a trace of what it means to push against authority, but neither film takes up adequately what it might mean to name and struggle against institutional practices within rather than outside of history, politics, and power. While the students response to *Stand and Deliver* was taken up more critically because of its concerns with race, class, and identity, it raised once again the crucial issue of how desire is mobilized by film narratives.

In engaging these two films, it became clear to me that the binarism that often structures the relationship between meaning and pleasure was ruptured. Those students who initially took up either of the films in terms of a desired images of themselves as a future teacher reworked that particular image not by canceling out the importance of desire, but by extending its possibilities by developing a transformed sense of agency and power.

Reclaiming the Popular

Any attempt to reclaim the popular in the service of a critical pedagogical practice runs the risk of at least three serious reactionary interventions. First, the popular or everyday is often used by mainstream and liberal educators merely to reaffirm the textual authority of canonical texts. Second, humanistic discourses sometimes use the popular as if it were an unproblematic mode of discourse and style, as if student voices in and of themselves lend authority that needs no further discussion or analysis. Third, there is the risk of colonizing the popular in the interests of subordinating it to the discourse of pedagogical techniques.[14]

The category of cultural worker used throughout this chapter refigures the role of educators within a discourse that takes a subject position, a standpoint that argues that without a political project there can be no ground on which to engage questions of power, domination, and the possibilities of collective struggle. This suggests a political project that goes beyond merely discursive struggles. Such a project also attempts to transform non-discursive and institutional relations of power by connecting educational struggles with broader struggles for the democratization, pluralization, and reconstruction of public life. With all apologies to the new conservativism, this is not an endorsement of that strange "species" of discourse popularly known as political correctness but a refusal to erase the political as an essential sphere of pedagogical practice.

If the popular is not to be used to reassert the validity of dominant texts and power relations, it must be viewed as part of a broader process of cultural production that is inextricably linked to issues of power, struggle, and identity. In this case, the popular does not derive its importance as an exotic text brought in from the margins of everyday life. On the contrary, it is used to raise questions about how its exclusion from the centers of power serve to secure specific forms of authority. The political currency of popular culture is not to be determined within a binarism that simply reverses its relationship to high culture. The more important task for cultural workers is to reconstruct the very problematic that informs the high vs. popular culture distinction in order to understand more specifically how cultural production works within and outside of the margins of power in texts actively engaged in the production of institutional structures, social identities, and horizons of possibility. For example, educators might use films, videos, or television within an English class so as to draw attention to the relevance of certain canonical works for everyday life. This approach does not challenge canonicity, it merely serves to make it appear more relevant.

Another use of the popular rests with the assumption that the use of rock music, popular films, and current novels represents a discourse of authenticity that resonates with the "real" experiences that constitute student voices. This position not only wrongly posits experience as something that is free of contradictions but also treats students' voices as texts whose authenticity dispenses with the need to make them the object of critical interrogation, mediation, and theoretical inquiry. Paul Smith captures this sentiment well:

> Deriving from the liberal-progressivist educational tradition which reached its acme (or nadir) with the call to relevance in the late 1960's, whatever increased interest there is in [such texts] often leads teachers to use them to facilitate students in expressing or assessing their own experiences. The logic is that the nearest access that most students have to culture is through and in mass culture and that their interest and participation in that realm can be turned toward self-expression and self-consciousness. In this process, so the argument goes, students will see their own experiences reflected and thus be more satisfied with the classroom experience than if they were taught canonical texts (33).

What Smith is rightly criticizing is not only a prevailing form of anti-intellectualism, but also a view of pedagogy that romanticizes student experience by removing it from the historical, institutional, and discursive forces which shape it in multiple and contradictory ways. Moreover, such a discourse locates experience within an individualist ethos that renders its social grounds and collective obligations invisible. In this case, relativism overrides the concerns of social justice, and individual views outweigh the consequences of the actions that follow from them on the broader public sphere. Finally, it is important to resist the pedagogical practice of treating the cultural text solely as an ever-expanding site of meanings, interpretations, and translations. While the reading of any cultural text can be reduced to the bad faith of textual essentialism or the one right meaning and must be avoided, it is imperative to recognize that popular texts must be read differently and politically; the readings of cultural texts must be understood within the larger dynamics of historical and social formations that struggle over such texts as sites of meaning and possibility.[15] Similarly, both cultural texts and the readings that circulate within, above, and against them must be examined as part of a broader discourse that takes up the circuits of power that constitute the ideological and material dynamics of capitalism (or any other social and economic system).

Conclusion

Rather than assuming that the popular is simply out there beyond the margins of disciplinary knowledge, ensconced in the play of everyday life waiting to be rescued as a serious object of knowledge, I want to conclude by addressing more directly the relationship between pedagogical authority and the appropriation of popular texts such as Hollywood films. Put another way, how can a notion of pedagogical authority be used to justify engaging what is problematically constituted as the popular in the first place? To be sure, it is important for cultural workers to use pedagogical authority in an emancipatory fashion to engage popular culture, to question and unlearn the benefits of privilege, and to allow those who have generally not been allowed to speak to narrate themselves, to speak from the specificity of their own voices. At the same time, it is in the service of reactionary interests for teachers and students to redefine authority as a legitimating discourse that opens up dialogue around the terrain of popular culture, but in doing so fails to interrogate how the dynamics of race, class, and gender, in particular, structure pedagogical projects in which everyday life is appropriated as part of a wider politics of containment. Needless to say, this does not always happen without struggle or resistance, but the issue here is how does one locate oneself as a cultural worker or educator within a notion of authority that legitimates engaging particular forms of popular texts without committing at the same time a form of pedagogical terrorism. How does one legitimate a notion of pedagogical authority that does not justify forms of voyeurism, looking, and appropriation that mimic the legacy of colonialism?

Raising this postcolonial caveat is not meant to suggest that progressive and left cultural workers who take up a directive notion of authority locate themselves by default in the discourse and practice of authoritarianism. On the contrary, authority needs to be reworked and struggled over as part of a wider effort to develop the pedagogical conditions necessary to make the invisible visible, expose how power is mobilized in the interests of oppression, and challenge the very terms of dominant representations. This suggests a notion of authority, popular culture, and pedagogical practice that combines a discourse of hope with forms of self- and social criticism while reclaiming a politics of location that recognizes how power, history, and ethics position, limit, and enable the cultural practices we engage in as educators. At issue here is an emancipatory notion of authority that should be fashioned in pedagogical practices rewritten in terms that articulate the importance of creating the conditions for students to take up subject positions consistent with the principles of equality, justice, and freedom rather than with interests and practices supportive of hierarchies, oppression, and exploitation. Central to this notion of authority is the need for critical educators to develop those spaces and practices that engage but don't erase the identities, compassion, or willingness of students to challenge the discourses of authority. The legitimation for such authority is as self-critical as it is deeply political, multi-accentual as it is committed to working within and across cultural and social differences to produce the basis for diverse critical public cultures that expand rather than restrict a democratic society.

To reclaim the popular within a committed view of authority is not meant to smother students under the weight of a suffocating form of political correctness. On the contrary, it is to engage the popular as part of a broader circuit of power relations, assert multiple notions of subjectivity without erasing agency, and expand the possibilities of multiple readings of texts while making visible how representations work so as to mobilize both the dynamics of domination and emancipatory struggles. In addition, there is the need for cultural workers to expand the boundaries of historical and semiotic analyses by making the pedagogical more political by addressing and transforming the conditions that will undermine relations of domination while simultaneously creating spaces of resistance, collective struggle, and hope.

Notes

1   For a theoretical analysis of the depoliticizing nature of aesthetic discourse, principally as it has been used by Marxists, see Bennett (1985). For an analysis of the depoliticizing of politics, see Grossberg (forthcoming).

2   I have taken this issue up in Giroux, *Border Crossings* (1992).

3   This issue is taken this issue up in great detail in Aronowitz and Giroux (1991).

4   This issue is explored from a variety of contexts in Ferguson, et. al. (1991) See Hall (1989) for an analysis of the relationship between culture and politics as part of the new hegemonic thrust in England.

5   Giroux and Trend (forthcoming) provide a critical analysis of the conservative assault on education and the arts in the United States.

6   For three excellent collections that address these issues in feminist, postmodern, and postcolonial terms, see Grossberg, Nelson, and Treichler, eds.;   Rutherford, ed.(1991); Ferguson, Gever, Minh-ha, and West, eds. (1991)

7   The chief proponent of this position is Graff (1990).   As Bruce Henricksen (1990) points out, Graff does not sufficiently "contextualize his model as a class and power-allocating activity"; nor does he move beyond the relativism of a dialogic model in which there is "no firm ground, nothing to believe in but the conversation itself." (pp. 31, 35).

8   The theoretical rationale and specifics of this type of critical pedagogy, one which is linked to the imperatives of defining teachers as transformative intellectuals, and pedagogy as a broader exercise in the creation of critical citizens can be found in Giroux, *Schooling and the Struggle for Public Life* (1988).

9   For an exemplary analysis of critical pedagogy as a form of cultural politics, see Simon (1992).

10   On the radical need to engage "whiteness" as a central racial category in the construction of moral power and political/cultural domination, see Dyer (1998); West, "The New Cultural Politics" 105 (1990); Ferguson, et. al. (1991)

11   For another analysis of the relationship between critical pedagogy and the issue of resistance in *Dead Poets Society*, see Peter McLaren (1991).

12   There is a curious "structuring silence" in Keating's refusal to engage or indicate any evidence of the "beat" literature of the 1950s, which appropriated "carpe diem" as a "counter-cultural text. Given Keating's hip, iconoclastic pedagogy, it seems inconceivable that a "free thinking" English teachers would not be aware of the works of "beat" poets and novelist such as Jack Kerouac, William Burroughs, Gregory Corso, Allen Ginsberg, and others.

13   I would like to thank Hilary Radner for her comments about gender relations in this film.

14   I have taken up this issue particularly with respect the appropriation of Paulo Freire's work and the pedagogy of the popular, see Giroux "Paulo Freire and the Politics of Post-colonialism;" see also the various articles in Giroux and Simon (1989).

15   For an excellent analysis of the politics of reading formations, see Tony Bennett, *Outside Literature*.

3.

Rewriting the Politics of Identity and Difference

Critical Pedagogy Without Illusions

I want to begin by quoting two teachers, both of whom harbor strong feelings and passions about the issue of multiculturalism and race. The first quote is by the late James Baldwin, the renowned Afro-American writer. The second quote recently appeared in *The Chronicle of Higher Education* and is by Melvin E. Bradford, a former speech writer for George Wallace and, more recently, an editorial writer working on behalf of former Republican presidential candidate Patrick Buchanan:

> If...one managed to change the curriculum in all the schools so that [Afro-Americans] learned more about themselves and their real contributions to this culture, you would be liberating not only [Afro-Americans], you'd be liberating white people who know nothing about their own history. And the reason is that if you are compelled to lie about one aspect of anybody's

history, you must lie about it all. If you have to lie
about my real role here, if you have to pretend that I
hoed all that cotton just because I loved you, then you
have done something to yourself. You are mad.[1]

I am not a scientific racist...But blacks as a group have
been here a long time and, for some reason, making
them full members of our society has proven almost
impossible. They remain outside. The more privileges
black Americans have had, the worse they seem to do.
At the core of it is black private life-those things we
can't legislate and can't control....I have a deep
suspicion that in matters that affect the course of their
lives, blacks habitually shoot themselves in the foot.[2]

What these quotes suggest in the most benign sense is that
issues concerning multiculturalism are fundamentally about questions
of race and identity. A less sanguine analysis reveals what both of
these quotes share, but what only Baldwin is willing to name: that
multiculturalism is not only about the discourse of alleged others but it
is also fundamentally about the issue of whiteness as a mark of racial
and gender privilege. For example, Baldwin argues that
multiculturalism cannot be reduced to an exclusive otherness that
references Afro-Americans, Hispanics, Latinos, or other suppressed
minorities, as either a problem to be resolved through the call for
benevolent assimilation or as a threat to be policed and eliminated. For
Baldwin, multiculturalism is primarily about whiteness and its claims
to a self definition that excludes itself from the messy relations of race,
ethnicity, power, and identity. On the other hand, Bradford exemplifies
a dominant approach to multiculturalism that serves as a coded
legitimation for equating of racial, cultural, and ethnic diversity with
social chaos, the lowering of standards, and the emergence of an
alleged new tribalism that threatens the boundaries of a common
culture or national identity. What both of these positions highlight is
how differences in power and privilege mediate who speaks, under
what conditions and for whom. In this sense, multiculturalism raises

the question of whether people are speaking within or outside a privileged space, and whether such spaces provide the conditions for different groups to listen to each other differently in order to address how the racial economies of privilege and power work in this society.

I want to argue that in the aftermath of the L. A. uprising educators need to rethink the politics of multiculturalism as part of a broader attempt to understand how issues regarding national identity, culture, and ethnicity can be rewritten in order to enable dominant groups to examine, acknowledge, and unlearn their own privilege. In part this demands an approach to the discourse of identity that not only addresses "the context of massive black unemployment, overcrowded schools, a lack of recreational facilities, dilapidated housing and racist policing,"[3] but a concerted attempt to view most racism in this country not as an issue of black lawlessness but primarily as an expression of white 'supremacy.'"[4] More specifically, a critical approach to cultural difference must shift attention away from an exclusive focus on subordinate groups, especially since such an approach tends to highlight their deficits, to one which examines how racism in its various forms is produced historically, semiotically, and institutionally at various levels of society. In opposition to a quaint liberalism, cultural difference means more than simply acknowledging "others" and analyzing stereotypes, more fundamentally it means understanding, engaging, and transforming the diverse institutions that produce racism and other forms of discrimination.

It is worth noting that in the aftermath of the recent Los Angeles uprising many educational commentators have ruled out any discussion of about the relationship between race and class and how they are manifested within networks of hierarchy and subordination both in and out of the schools. This particular silence when coupled with the popular perception that the L.A. uprising can be explained by pointing to those involved as simply thugs, looters, and criminals makes it clear why the multicultural peril is often seen as a black threat; it also suggests what such a belief shares with the traditionalists view of the "other" as a disruptive outsider. In this scenario, cultural differences and multiculturalism become the source of the problem.

Modernism and the Politics of Difference

> At the end of the 20th century, U.S. society is
> becoming more racially and ethnically diverse; more
> polarized along class lines; more alarmed by lesbians,
> gay men, and other sexual minorities; more conscious
> of gender differences; and, as a result, increasingly
> preoccupied with [the politics of identity]....This
> politics of identity is a kind of cultural politics. It relies
> on the development of a culture that is able to create
> new and affirmative conceptions of the self, to
> articulate collective identities, and to forge a sense of
> group loyalty. In identity politics...there is a strong
> emphasis on inventing a new language and a new
> vocabulary. But..identity politics also requires the
> development of rigid definitions of the boundaries
> between those who share particular collective identities
> and those who do not.[5]

Within the last decade, the concept of identity has moved to the
center of debates around issues concerning community, culture, and
difference. While the debates surrounding the struggle over identity
have surfaced with great forcefulness, the circumstances and contours
of this struggle are rooted historically in a series of conditions that
have come to constitute what I want to call the crisis of modernism.[6]

Central to this crisis are the emergence of new economic and
technological forces on the world order along with new social
movements and forms of cultural criticism that have unsettled some of
modernism's most cherished assumptions regarding identity and
culture.[7] These assumptions include modernism's emphasis on the
mutually reinforcing categories of the unified and autonomous self and
the construction of culture as synonymous with the most basic tenets of
Western European civilization.

In the first instance, modernism defined the relationship among
identity, culture, agency, and community in ways that reinforced rather

than challenged existing networks of hierarchy and exploitation. The modernist construction of the humanist subject, despite the legacy of Marx, Freud, and Nietzsche, often ignored how individuals were constructed within complex, multilayered, and contradictory social formations. At the same time, the autonomous self became the most important unit of analysis in understanding human agency, freedom, and politics. Anchored in the notion of a static and unified identity, the conceptions of subjectivity and freedom were organized around the theory of a free and independent individual. Within this ideological matrix, the freedom and autonomy characteristic of the self-contained subject became the ideological referent for defining choice as the measure of freedom in the capitalist marketplace. In this version of modernism, the logic of the marketplace narrowly defined the parameters of freedom for both human agency and the larger sphere of democracy itself.[8] Missing from this discourse was any analysis of those social and political forces that constructed individual and collective identities across and within different economic, cultural, and social spheres.

Lost here was any acknowledgment or account of the pluralization and diversification of positions and identities available to people struggling over expanding claims to rights, redefining the terms of membership in the dominant society, and rewriting the rules of participation in the creation of multiple democratic public cultures and communities. Moreover, within this discourse the conception of agency as plural, subversive, and constitutive of social movements was rendered invisible. Instead of recognizing multiple, collective agents capable of both challenging existing configurations of power and offering new visions of the future, modernism constructed a politics of identity within the narrow parameters of an individualism that was fixed, unburdened by history, and free from the constraints of multiple forms of domination.

Understood in these terms, modernism constructed a notion of identity through an ideology of individualism that erased the concept of the social as a viable political category. Within modernist discourses, social problems were often rewritten as individual dilemmas or subjective preferences; and those ideologies that threatened to challenge the status quo were similarly relegated to the depoliticized wasteland of the psychological. Displacing the social and political as primary forces in the construction of different subjects and individual identities, modernism relegated difference to the realm of either deviance and pathology or reduced its presence to the narrow arena of the private sphere.

Modernism's second basic assumption was grounded in the attempt to construct cultural differences within a discourse that was simultaneously ethnocentric, colonialist, and anti-democratic. In reproducing the discourse of ethnocentricism, modernism reinvented the discourse of colonialism by continually attempting to rework culture as an integrative category that served to either assimilate, ignore, or actively transform subaltern cultural traditions. Within the discourse of assimilation, difference was recognized only to be labelled as inferior and then reconstituted as part of the Western canon. The colonial legacy of modernism revealed itself with a vengeance in its aggressive policy of acknowledging cultural differences only to ultimately reinscribe them as part of a larger project of cultural containment.   In this case, various cultural traditions were either written out of history, made invisible, or marginalized. Similarly, emergent or resisting subordinate or minority traditions were actively modified intellectually, ideologically, and ethically so as to be re-constituted in ways that inextricably changed the composition of these identities, while at the same time making them complicitous with dominant European cultural traditions. Moreover, the anti-democratic nature of modernism pitted high culture against democracy in defense of an elitism that buttressed structural and ideological inequalities. Reasserting the appeal to "the best" of western culture, modernism's characteristic disdain of the popular was extended to the sphere of democracy itself. Samuel Lipman, a leading contemporary spokesperson for neo-conservatism articulates the anti-democratic parameters of this tradition very well:

> Culture and democracy cannot co-exist, for democracy
> by its very nature represents the many, and culture, by
> its nature, is created for the few. What the many

cannot immediately comprehend, they destroy; what
the few cannot directly control, they reject....What is
necessary are definitions of culture and democracy
based...less on inclusions and more on exclusions.[9]

In all of these instances, modernism promoted a theory of
culture defined by nostalgic appeals to the past and the importance of
cultural frontiers that invoked a view of safety and comfort while
simultaneously policing and incorporating "those who were potential
threats to [the dominant] culture."[10]

Increasingly, radical notions of identity have contested the
material, symbolic, and imagined boundaries of subjectivity and
cultural difference as they have been constructed within modernist
discourses that regulated conservative and liberal political ideologies.
As part of a broader struggle over identity politics, a number of
diverse groups during the 1960s attempted to rethink and assert their
political and cultural identities within rather than outside of specific
racial, sexual, and gender categories. Challenging the notion of class as
an exhaustive category for defining the narrative of location and
change, blacks rewrote the discourse of identity within the cultural and
political parameters of the black power movement. At the same time,
women were asserting a new relationship among politics, experience,
and identity by organizing within a second generation of feminist
struggles. Similarly, gay and lesbian activists affirmed the right to
sexual freedom by organizing powerful social movements. More
recently, we have witnessed the resurgence of a number of subaltern
groups, informed by the changing conditions of a postcolonial and
postmodern world, who are attempting to rewrite their histories and
experiences as a way of reclaiming power and identity.[11]

Cornell West has argued that the present cultural crisis and the
emergence of new social movements is rooted both in a series of
processes associated, in part, with the decolonization of the Third
World, and in the production of new forms of social criticism that
challenge the authority, representations, and values the Western world
has used to sustain dominating and coercive colonial institutions and
social relations.[12] Unlike many of the previous discourses that have

addressed issues of difference and power, many of the theorists promoting what West has called the new cultural politics of difference draw heavily from the disciplinary boundaries of poststructuralism, postmodernism, and feminist theory in order to create a "third space" for analyzing the politics of identity. At stake here is an attempt to make visible not only how traditional notions of identity reproduce forms of domination and oppression, but also to illuminate how the politics of identity and difference have both advanced and undermined the possibilities for new, emancipatory political movements. At its best, the new politics of cultural difference goes far beyond offering a new twist on critically analyzing identity politics. If this is all it did, the new politics of cultural difference would not have much to offer. In fact, the literature on difference and identity has become something of a boom industry and is much too extensive to cite here.[13] The new politics of cultural difference not only provides a new space for retrieving and reconstructing history through "a critical redeployment of imagination....able to discriminate between reality as fact and existence as possibility,"[14] it also offers a new discourse, in an era marked by major economic, cultural, and political transformations, for extending and deepening the possibilities for a radical-democratic politics.

It is worth noting that critical educators and workers who are grappling with forging a cultural politics that rewrites the connection between identity politics and the discourse of democracy, citizenship, and ethics need a new language in which to reinsert the notion of social struggle into the discourse of hope and possibility. Such a language needs to take seriously the attempt to reconcile difference and community as central to the project of reconstructing a critical democracy. Central to such a language is the dual dynamics of deconstruction and productive struggle. Educators need more than a language of critique, they also need a language of possibility in which the concerns of Ernesto Laclau and Chantal Mouffe can be taken seriously. They write: "if the demands of [the left] are presented purely as negative demands subversive of a certain order, without being linked to any viable project for the reconstruction of specific areas of society, their capacity to act hegemonically will be excluded from the outset."[15]

In what follows, I want to analyze the politics of identity and difference through the lens of three registers. First, I want to address how the right wing in the United States has situated the issue of identity and difference within the dynamics of domination, hierarchy, and racism. Second, I want to analyze some of the theoretical and political problems that have emerged within the discourse of difference and identity politics. Finally, I want to take up the issue of developing a language of articulation in which difference and unity mutually inform each other as part of a broader discourse of freedom and democracy. I will conclude by pointing out some of the implications a politics of identity and differences has for pedagogy as a form of cultural politics.

Neo-Conservatism and the Politics of Identity

The crisis in modernism has not only spurned the emergence of a new politics of identity and cultural difference, it has also mobilized a right wing counter offensive. This is most evident in the current conservative attack on multiculturalism, cultural difference, school curricula, the arts, civil rights legislation, and the democratization of the academic canon.[16] In effect, the right has attempted to respond to new social divisions, movements, and the mobilizing potential of a radical, multicultural movement by extending modernism's attempt to obliterate or reincorporate those world views that challenge its most fundamental hegemonic assumptions.

The importance of the issue of identity politics may have less to do with how various left and progressive groups have used it as a rallying point to promote a particular political agenda within the last three decades than it does with the intensity of the attack that is currently being waged against multiculturalism, cultural differences, and the politics of identity by conservative and right wing groups, particularly in the United States and England. By producing diverse forms of cultural criticism within a vast array of public spheres, the proponents of identity politics both questioned the "unspoken assumption of white, male, heterosexual identity, which underlies the concept of the 'universal'"[17] and undermined the hegemonic world view constructed by the Reagan and Thatcher administrations in the 1980s. Advocates of the new politics of cultural difference also made visible and challenged how the politics of representation and institutional power work to secure right-wing authority. Postmodern, postcolonial and feminist discourses dramatically revealed how dominant texts served to erase, marginalize, and determine the way in which identities are represented in the wider society. In so doing, they began to produce a critical ethnography of the west that placed issues of knowledge, power, and voice as foreground to the issue of who has the power to politically represent, speak, and act on behalf of others.[18]

While it has become increasingly fashionable for certain groups on both the left and right to focus on the dangers of identity politics, a number of cultural critics view the right wing attack against cultural difference as the most serious issue facing not only subordinate groups but the very nature of democracy itself.[19] This is not meant to suggest that these critics do not recognize or address the many problems and limitations that have traditionally beset identity politics. On the contrary, the new discourse of cultural difference offers a number of excellent critiques of the limitations of the existing politics of identity and cultural difference. But rather than simply dismissing the current limitations of left wing identity politics, these authors begin with the recognition that the right wing attack on cultural difference must be seen as the starting point for developing transformative aspects of a cultural politics that promotes rather than undermines the potential of radical democratic life.

Central to this argument is the need for progressive individuals to use identity politics as a rallying point for engaging contemporary, right wing attacks against cultural difference. The concept of identity politics should be reformulated and reproblematized as part of a broader attempt to analyze how the dynamics of cultural power work within the classical economy of language, representation, and institutional structures to position "a subject or set of peoples as the other of a dominant discourse."[20] At issue here, as Rosalind Brunt, states is the need to recognize that "unless the question of identity is at the heart of any transformative project, then not only will the political agenda be inadequately 'rethought', but more to the point, our politics aren't going to make much headway beyond the Left's own circles."[21]

Rather than abandoning the issue of identity politics, the new radical discourse on difference wants to reformulate it as part of a broader attack on the right wing conception of history, nationalism, and patriotism, while simultaneously rearticulating identity and cultural difference as central elements in progressive debates around democracy, citizenship, and social justice. In other words, the new cultural politics of difference situates the notion of identity and culture as a critical referent for understanding how the right wing is engaging in a full fledged assault on the foundations of democratic public life. But equally important is that it addresses in new terms how the problems facing radical proponents of cultural difference might provide the opportunity for reformulating a politics of identity outside of the dictates of a narrow separatism and essentialism. In fact, an overriding theme of this perspective is that it is necessary for left and progressive cultural workers to understand the nature of the threat that the right-wing has mobilized against the issues of cultural difference and multiculturalism in order to move beyond the current political impasse of identity politics.

Beset by the assertion of new ethnicities, the proliferation of global and cultural identities, and the rewriting of the public sphere within the discourses of hybridity and heterogeneity, conservatives feel besieged.[22] Lacking the courage to rework dominant traditions in light of a changing present and future, conservatives continue to develop "imaginary unities" aimed at creating rigid cultural boundaries that serve to seize upon fear and cultural racism. Rutherford expands this theme and argues that conservatives utilize a two pronged attack against difference. In the first instance, the Right promises "strong defenses and well-policed frontiers against the transgressive threat and displacements of difference. Even as it claims the universal nature of its constituent identities, its struggle to maintain the cultural, sexual and racial dichotomies of Self and Other make and reproduce social formations of domination and inequality."[23] Rutherford adds an insightful twist to the second strategy used by conservatives to control and displace cultural differences. In this case, difference is translated into a commodity relation and "otherness is sought after for its exchange value, its exoticism and the pleasures, thrills and adventures it can offer. The power relation is closer to tourism than imperialism, an expropriation of meaning rather than materials."[24]   In both cases, conservatives attempt to depoliticize difference by inserting it in a power-neutral discourse. Whether the appeal is to an imaginary unity allegedly free of ideological interests or to a commodity designed to promote pleasure and consumption, difference is delegitimated as a terrain of political struggle and contestation.   The deadly paradox in the conservative offensive is constructed around a politics of difference that attempts to depoliticize politics while simultaneously politicizing culture. Differences in the first instance is assigned to either the realm of the aesthetic or to the harmonizing discourse of cultural diversity which serves to "locate cultures in a universal time-frame that acknowledges their various historical and social contexts only eventually to transcend them and render them transparent." [25]   Critics such as Homi Bhabha and Chandra Mohanty have deepened and extended this critique by arguing that cultural diversity, as opposed to the more power-sensitive discourse of cultural difference, serves to contain issues of identity, culture, and agency within the harmonizing discourse of consensus, common culture, and national unity.[26]

On the other hand, as I mentioned previously, the right wing has attempted to politicize culture by waging a massive assault on schools, the arts, and health care programs. Consequently, within the last decade there have been drastic cutbacks in public services, an ongoing attempt by conservatives to replace state provision and public service with privatization programs designed to expand the power of capital, individual competitiveness, and corporate freedom. One result has been a redistribution of wealth from the poor to the rich, an expansion of the web of poverty to the point where 25 percent of all children currently live below the poverty level, and the emergence of growing acts of racism in a variety of public spheres. Faced with the legacy of postcolonial struggles, struggles over individual and national identities, conservatives have resorted to mobilizing forms of national hatred, racism, and assaults on civil rights. Given the current offensive by conservatives against difference and democracy, many progressive cultural critics have argued that the left politics of identity and cultural difference are inappropriate as a political strategy for the 1990s. Ellen Willis provides a severe but insightful critique of the theoretical and political dead end in which identity politics found itself in the 1970s and 1980s and the legacy she believes must be challenged in the 1990s.

> The appeal of "identity politics" is that it arises from a radical insight-that domination is systematically structured into the relations between social groups. The problem is that it gives rise to a logic that chokes off radicalism and ends up by supporting domination. If the present obsession with group identity as the basis for politics is hard to imagine, much less build, a broad-based radical collectivity, it has even more tellingly stood in the way of a principled commitment to the freedom and happiness of individuals, without which no genuine radicalism is possible.[27]

In spite of the emerging criticism, issues of identity have begun to occupy the center of academic and popular debates around issues concerning culture, difference, and democratic renewal. But before addressing what the re-emergence of identity politics suggests for a cultural politics and radical pedagogy in the 1990s, I want to point more specifically to some of the problems of identity politics as it emerged in the last three decades.

The Difficulty of Difference

The problems with identity politics cannot be separated from the failure of the old and new left to recognize that identity is "not reducible to the single logic of class."[28] Kobena Mercer address this issue and argues that the very ambiguity of identity, in which the individual can no longer be viewed as an undifferentiated, whole, stable, and autonomous self, served as a way of not only acknowledging new social actors and new political subjects, but also undermining the "totalizing universal truth claims of ideologies like Marxism, thus demanding acknowledgment of the plural sources of oppression, unhappiness and antagonism in contemporary capitalist societies."[29] If the old left of orthodox Marxism reduced complex, social relations to the determinations of economic materialism, the new left of the 1960s and 70s recognized the autonomy of different social movements as they emerged within the politics of race, sexuality and gender. Unfortunately, new left groups were "unable to think through the formation of people and their identities within a number of relationships, for example, race and class, simultaneously. Nor could [the new left] cope with the complexities of difference both within and between social movements."[30] The identity politics of the 1980s and early 90s never recovered from the theoretical impasse it reached in the 1970s. Identity politics was soon under siege by black feminists who rejected the racism and discourse of authenticity that characterized a largely white, middle class, feminist movement that claimed to speak for all women.[31] Mercer builds upon these positions to argue that identity politics eventually degenerated into the worse kind of essentialism. He is worth quoting at length on this issue:

> The worst aspects of the new social movement emerged in a rhetoric of 'identity politics' based on an essentialist notion of a fixed hierarchy of racial, sexual or gendered oppressions. By playing off each other to establish who was more authentically oppressed than whom, the residual separatist tendencies of the autonomous movement played into the normative calculation of 'disadvantage' inscribed in welfare statism....as the various actors perceived it, one group's loss was another group's gain. In this zero-sum game the only tangible consequence of diversity was dividedness.[32]

Within this perspective, the discourses of authenticity, experience, and the personal exceeded whatever liberatory potential they might have had and "the authority of someone's politics was affirmed by whatever category of oppression they belonged to. Political moralism came to police the boundaries of identities, encouraging uniformity and ensuring intellectual inertia."[33] Analyzing the essentialism and the over-privileging of experience that has characterized mainstream, Western feminist theory, Patribha Parmar argues insightfully that "whereas the problem of women's liberation was once how to assert personal issues as political, the problem has now reversed to one where feminists need to argue that the political does not reduce to the personal."[34]

It is important to stress that the discourse of authenticity is alive and well in the vocabularies of various social movements, especially in educational circles. Within this discourse, the politics of personal location has become the new ideological litmus test for revealing the authenticity of one's politics. Texts now are interrogated by exposing the master narratives that allegedly lurk behind the hidden experiences and identities of the author(s) who produce them. The task is no longer to make clear the ideology that informs one's position; one has to now genuflect before the discourse of the "authentic experience" in order to be taken seriously. The "new" politics of experience is questionable on a number of grounds. To accept the authority of experience uncritically is to forget that identity itself is complex, contradictory, and multilayered. Any simple correspondence between experience and the theoretical and political weight of a particular position is simply not tenable. Simply put, one always runs the danger of essentialism and separatism by ignoring that "the politics of any social position is not guaranteed in advance."[35] Moreover, the emphasis on the personal as the fundamental aspect of the political often results in highlighting the personal through a form of "confessional" politics that all but forgets how the political is constituted in social and cultural forms outside of one's own experience. Moreover, alliances often developed around the alleged authenticity of particular experiences often forget, as June Jordan points out in an interview with Patribha Parmar, "that partnership in misery does not necessarily provide for partnership for change."[36]

The discourse of authenticity, essentialism, and separatism also strongly influenced a politics of representation that was bent on discovering lost histories as part of an attempt to recover a "real" and authentic historical experience. Utilizing the metaphor of "home" as a place one can never return to again, Stuart Hall argues that all identities are subject to the shifting movement and 'play' of history, culture, and power. Identities undergo constant transformations, and in doing so make problematic the act of imaginative rediscovery which the search for hidden histories entail. But rather than dismissing the relationship between history, identity, and memory, Hall situates it in an entirely different problematic. He writes:

> Is it only a matter of unearthing that which the colonial experience buried and overlaid, bringing to light the hidden continuities it suppressed? Or is a quite different practice entailed-not the rediscovery but the *production* of identity. Not an identity grounded in the archaeology, but in the *re-telling* of the past.[37]

Towards a Politics of Articulation

Not only does the new politics of cultural difference present an argument for recognizing that the issue of cultural and political identity needs to be rethought rather than abandoned, it also makes the related issues of difference and identity central to the discourse of democracy, politics, and agency. In doing so, it offers educators a new language for retheorizing how cultural identities are constantly being reworked and transformed within differences negotiated through the play of history, memory, language, and power. It also points to how the discourse of difference can be used to rewrite the social contract between groups in ways that deepen and extend the possibility for a democratic community. Central to the new politics of cultural difference is the need for cultural workers and educators to develop a new vocabulary that gives the relationship between unity and difference a political project, one that promotes contemporary alliances among oppositional groups. In more general terms, the central question at stake here is how to promote forms of "democratic representation and participation that would be responsive to the diversity of social identities active in the contemporary polity." [38]

Jeffrey Weeks argues that the answer rests in part in the creation of a set of principles based on the acceptance and necessity for a political community that makes diversity central to the meaning of democracy. For Weeks, this means that educators and other cultural workers need to develop a concept of critical citizenship informed by a set of values that embraces the pluralization of democratic rights, entitlements, and obligations as part of the wider discourse of agency and ethics. Without imitating an all embracing humanism, Weeks wants progressives to acknowledge the shifting nature of identity, while not eliminating the issue of human agency; at the same time, he wants them to expand the basis for dialogue and community without erasing a politics of difference. He writes:

> We may not be able to find, indeed we should not seek, a single way of life that would satisfy us all. That does not mean we cannot agree on common political ends: the construction of what can best be described as a 'community of communities', to achieve a maximum political unity without denying difference. [39]

For Weeks the intersection of difference and identity is a marker not only for one's sense of location, a shifting narrative of identifications that provides a conception of individuality, but also a dialogic process in which the issue of self representation is constituted in our relationship with others. Hence, as Stuart Hall points out:

> The critical thing about identity is that it is partly the relationship between you and the Other. Only when there is an Other can you know who you are....And there is no identity...without the dialogic relationship to the Other. The Other is not outside, but also inside the Self, the identity. So identity is a process, identity is split. Identity is not a fixed point but an ambivalent

point. Identity is also the relationship of the Other to oneself.[40]

For Weeks and Hall, the issues of identity and difference point to a rethinking of both the discourse of ethics and representation, while simultaneously seeking a fresh understanding of how to "imagine" new forms of political community outside of the existing configuration of the liberal nation state.

Homi Bhabha reiterates this theme by arguing that the issues of hybridity and cultural translation open up a "third space" where it becomes possible to challenge the modernist construction of history, progress, the myth of the nation, and ethnocentricism which lie at the heart of the construction of Western civil societies. Hybridity does not merely suggest that all forms of culture are related, it also challenges the great structuring principles of modernism by accentuating the emergence of new global subjects, diasporic communities, and border identities. Bhabha's "third space" provides a new theoretical marker which "enables other positions to emerge. This "third space" displaces the histories that constitute it, and sets up new structures of authority, new political initiatives, which are inadequately understood through received wisdom....This process of cultural hybridity gives rise to something different, something new and unrecognizable, a new area of negotiation of meaning and representation."[41] Bhabha's notions of hybridity and cultural translation do more than authenticate different histories, they offer the promise of exposing and interrogating the colonial face of modernity while simultaneously calling forth new sites of political negotiation, sites which displace dominant terms of negotiation and in doing so rewrite the possibility for creating critical public spheres, such as schools and other social spheres where politics and pedagogy unite to:

> open up an interaction or a dialogism of the powerful,
> the powerless, and its is this site--which enables
> another distribution of meaning, a change in the ratio
> of powers, because neither of the two settled moments

prior to this hybrid site are imported into it in their previous form.[42]

Conclusion

One of the most important challenges facing critical educators is to address the emerging complex, politics of identity in political and pedagogical terms that refuse the "comfortable" discourses of essentialism and separatism. This means rewriting the relationship among identity, culture, and difference so as to address how, for example, race, class, and gender can be analyzed in their historically specific interrelationships. The structuring principles of identity politics loose their power when they are taken up outside of the complex historical and relational practices that position people within a variety of subject positions. More specifically, identity politics suggest that educators need to be attentive to the necessity of developing a pedagogy of place. In part, such a pedagogy refuses the safety of occupied theoretical territory, the determinism of master narratives, and the cynicism that relegates teachers to a place outside of power and struggle. A pedagogy of place is always attentive to what Lemuel Johnson calls the "density of specification,"[43] that is, those particular histories, experiences, languages and cultural memories which offer the conditions for an insurgent subjectivity. Similarly, a pedagogy of place points to the need for cultural workers to reinvent and reconstruct new spaces for engaging critical pedagogy as an ever-becoming relation of theory and practice. In this instance, the relationship between theory and practice must focus not simply on the pedagogy of identity formation, but also on addressing how structures of inequality and injustice can be understood and transformed. Central to such a position is creating a discourse of agency, one which recognizes that the problem is not the geography of multiple subject positions that students inhabit, but how students actually negotiate them within a geography of desire, affect, and rationality.

In addition, a radical notion of identity politics points to the necessity for educators to become more self conscious and reflective about their own cultural and political locations. To do so is not to merely engage in "confessional" politics, but to make clear the power, limits, partiality, and indeterminacy of the sites which inscribe and enable one's sense of place, identity, and possibilities for action. What is called for in this case is a pedagogy without illusions, one which suggest that educators be scrupulous in turning the tools of dialogue and self-criticism upon their own work. Such a pedagogy suggests that educators and cultural workers cannot be content to be in one discourse. Critical educators have to become border crossers, allowing the focus of their analysis to shift, move, circle back on itself, and push against its own discourse so as to extend and deepen its implications for critical pedagogy while tracing out a recognizable shape of the complexity that informed its underlying project. A pedagogy of place makes no claims for an essentialist discourse of authenticity. In fact, it presents itself as an argument against such a logic.

While it is important for everyone to unlearn, within different degrees of power and oppression, the multiple forms of domination with which one might be complicit, it is also crucial to make questions of democracy central to the emancipatory project that informs our lives as cultural workers. This means developing a politics that reasserts the primacy of the social, incorporates multiple struggles, builds alliances, and recaptures the concept of solidarity as a central element of a pedagogy and politics of hope and possibility. More specifically, this suggests a number of practices. First, cultural workers need to examine the issue of cultural production and its relationship to texts, economies, institutions, audiences, and communities and how these social forms and the practices that inform them can be understood within and across the different circuits of power that characterize the wider society. In part, this can be done by focusing on pedagogy as an articulatory concept that provides a discourse of unity, one in which differences are not erased but linked within a set of unifying principles. Second, critical educators need to develop a new understanding of how teachers and other cultural workers can produce new cultural zones, public spheres, engage in new forms of cultural production, and address the challenges provided by multiple audiences. Once again, such a task suggests the need for critical educators to offer a new vision and space for re-writing not only the relationship between culture and power, identity and pedagogy, but also between cultural work and the project of democratic renewal. Let me be a bit more specific regarding these issues.

Central to the notion of critical pedagogy is the need to re-write the relationship among cultural and pedagogical production as part of a broader vision that extends the principles and practices of human dignity, liberty and social justice. In this view, the task of pedagogy is to deepen diverse democratic struggles which extend the ideological and material possibilities for self and collective determination across a broad range of economic, social, and political spheres. In part, this means taking up pedagogy as a form of cultural politics that addresses how different identities and experience get produced, and how they function in the broader community. At its best, critical pedagogy would establish the conditions to refigure a variety of human experiences within a discourse in which diverse political views, sexual orientations, races, ethnicities, and cultural differences can mutually co-exist amidst social relations that support free expression and uninhibited debate. In this case, cultural pedagogy is inseparable from cultural democracy. On one level this means deepening the political aspects of the pedagogical by providing equal access for cultural workers to the educational and cultural institutions that organize daily life; on another level, it means making the pedagogical more political by reconstructing the very concept of pedagogy as a social practice that generates new knowledge, opens up contradictions, and challenges all hierarchical structures of power that demand reverence at the expense of dialogue and debate.

With this qualification in mind, I want to stress that critical pedagogy as a theory and practice does not legitimate either a romanticized notion of the cultural worker who can only function on the margins of society, nor does it refer to a notion of teaching/cultural production in which methodological reification erases the historical, semiotic, and social dimensions of pedagogy as the active construction of responsible and risk-taking citizens.

The concept of cultural worker in its more narrow definition has generally been understood to refer to artists, writers, and media producers. Critical educators need to further develop the theoretical groundwork for extending the range of people associated with this term to others working in professions like law, social work, architecture, medicine, theology, education, and literature.[44]　By expanding the concept of cultural work and practice to include issues related to public philanthropy, media reception, town meetings, and popular education, critical educators can make a vital contribution to rewriting the cartography of innovation and struggle that such work involves and in doing so expands the spaces/locations and potential alliances from which the production of knowledge can be interrogated and reconstructed within the primacy of the political and the pedagogical.

The pedagogical dimension of cultural work refers to the process of creating symbolic representations and the practices within which they are engaged. This includes a particular concern with the analysis of textual, aural, and visual representations, and how such representations are organized and regulated within particular institutional arrangements. It also addresses how various people engage such representations in the practice of comprehension and significance. As a cultural practice, pedagogy both contests and refigures the construction, presentation, and engagement of various forms of images, text, talk, and action which results in the production of meaning, through which students construct their individual and collective futures. Pedagogy in this sense represents both a discourse of critique and a project of possibility.[45]

What is crucial to a critical pedagogy of place is the recognition that the political dimension of cultural work recognizes that the symbolic presentations which take place in various spheres of cultural production in society manifest contested and unequal power relations rooted in discursive and nondiscursive social forms. As a form of cultural production, pedagogy is implicated in the construction and organization of knowledge, desires, values, and social practices. It also serves to contest dominant forms of symbolic production. Cultural work, in this sense, informs a project whose intent is to mobilize knowledge and desires that may lead to significant changes in minimizing the degree of oppression in people's lives. What is at stake is a political imaginary which extends the possibilities for creating new public spheres and alliances in which the principles of equality, liberty, and justice become the primary organizing principles for not only structuring relationships between the self and others, but also for creating new social movements.

Critical educators also need to engage in what Stuart Hall calls "acts of cultural recovery."[46] This statement suggests that educators develop a pedagogical voice that goes beyond the task of discovering identities of Otherness as if they were self-contained, packaged, and ready to be unwrapped and named. It suggests the need for a pedagogical voice that demands the recovery of the complex traces of identity that mark dominant and subordinate groups through a critical reading of the way in which the relationship between the self and others is written and reworked within the shifting narratives of the past, present, and the future. By making difference and identity central to the spirit and experience of democratic learning, critical educators could take the offensive in the current debates on multicultural education by pointing to intolerance, not cultural differences as the enemy of democracy.

Finally, at the risk of repeating myself, critical educators and other cultural workers need to provide new theoretical elements for rethinking how the politics of cultural difference and identity advance the discourse of democracy. Central to such a project is the acknowledgment of the importance of struggling to create multiple public cultures. Such cultures need to be seen as critical spaces that offer the opportunity for diverse groups to engage in dialogue and exchange as part of a broader effort to make and remake their identities through an attempt to identity oneself with the suffering, actions, thoughts, and feelings of others. But there is more at stake here than simply developing an empathy for difference or an appreciation of the pleasure that can be produced in the discourse and relations of difference; there is also the need to struggle collectively around a politics of hope which envisions "the possibility of a society in which social equality and cultural diversity co-exist with participatory democracy."[47]

Notes

1   James Baldwin, "A Talk to Teachers." In Rick Simonson & Scott Walker, eds. *Multicultural Literacy: Opening the American Mind* (Saint Paul, Minnesota: Graywolf Press, 1988), p. 8.

2   Melvin E. Bradford quoted in Katherine S. Mangan, "6th Generation Texan Takes on 'Trendy Nonsense,' *The Chronicle of Higher Education* (July 8, 1992), p. A5.

3   Alan O'Connor, "Just Plain Home Cookin," *Borderlines*. N0s. 20/21 (Winter 1991), p. 58.

4   Marcia Tucker, "'Who's On First?' Issues of Cultural Equity in Today's Museums." In Carol Becker, et al. *Different Voices* (New York: Association of Art Museum Directors, 19920, p. 11.

5   Jeffrey Escoffier, "The Limits of Multiculturalism," *Socialist Review*, Vol. 91, Nos. 3 & 4 (July/December 1991), pp. 61-62.

6   I am well aware that the concept of modernism is open to enormous debate and little agreement. But I do not think that one risks theoretical credibility in arguing that modernism fundamentally depends upon humanism. Similarly, the crisis of modernism expresses itself in its inability to legitimate two central elements of its humanism: Eurocentrism as a organizing principle of the relationship between knowledge and power, and its advocacy of a view of agency rooted in a self-contained conception of the subject. It is also worth noting that the notion of the unified subject has been the object of attack by Marx, Freud, Nietzsche, Adorno, and others, but it is only within the last thirty years that this attack has gained ground on several analogous disciplinary and theoretical fronts. I take this issue up in great detail in Henry A. Giroux, *Border Crossings: Cultural Workers and the Politics of Education*. New York: Routledge, 1992.

7   In this case, I am referring to what Stuart Hall and others call the changing character of "new times," which includes the emergence of new information technologies, a

decline in the composition and character of the working class, an economies dominated by multinationals, the globalization of new financial markets, the decline of the nation state, and the development of an economy and culture dominated by service industries and consumerism. These categories are taken from: Stuart Hall, "The Meaning of New Times," in Stuart Hall and Martin Jacques, Eds., *New Times: The Changing Face of Politics in the 1990s*, London: Verso, 1990, pp. 116-133. For an analysis of the cultural and social changes characterizing "new times," see Cornel West, "The New Politics of Difference," *October*, No. 53 (Summer 1990), pp. 93-109.

[8] This issue is brilliantly discussed in Stanley Aronowitz, *The Crisis in Historical Materialism*. (Minneapolis: University of Minnesota Press, 1990) Especially chapter 8, pp. 256-303.

[9] Samuel Lipman, "Redefining Democracy and Culture," *New Criterion*, No. 8 (December 1989), p. 12.

[10] The notion of culture serving as a fortress against foreign threats is discussed in Cornel West, "Decentering Europe: A Memorial Lecture for James Snead," *Critical Inquiry*, Vol. 33, No. 1 (1991), pp. 7-8.

[11] This issue is taken up in great detail in both a variety of feminist and postcolonial discourses. For an overview of these various positions, see Henry A. Giroux, *Border Crossings: Cultural Workers and the Politics of Education*. New York: Routledge, 1992.

[12] See Cornel West, "The New Cultural Politics of Difference," *October* 53 (Summer 1990), pp. 93-109.

[13] For an overview and analysis of this literature, especially as it has been produced within the discourses of postmodernism, postcolonialism, and postfeminism, see Henry A. Giroux, *Border Crossings: Cultural Workers and the Politics of Education*, New York: Routledge, 1992.

[14] Richard Kearney, *Poetics of Imagining: From Husserl to Lyotard* (New York: Harper Collins, 1991), pp. 215-216.

15 Ernesto Laclau and Chantal Mouffe, *Hegemony & Socialist Strategy: Towards a Radical Democratic Politics*, trans. Winston Moore and Paul Cammack. London: Verso, 1985, p. 189.

16 For an superb, detailed analysis of these assaults, especially in the arts, see David Trend, *Cultural Pedagogy: Art/Politics/Theory*. New York: Bergin and Garvey, 1992.

17 Toni Morrison cited in Russell Ferguson, "Introduction: Invisible Center," Russell Ferguson, et. al. Eds. *Out There: Marginalization and Contemporary Cultures*. (Cambridge: MIT Press, 1990) p.10.

18 Rosalind Brunt, "The Politics of Identity," *New Times: The changing Face of Politics in the 1990s*, op. cit., p. 152.

19 While it is impossible to site all of the writers who are taking up identity politics in a critically transformative way, some of the more interesting examples include: bell hooks, *Yearnings*. Boston: South End Press, 1990; Michele Wallace, *Invisibility Blues: From Pop to Theory*. London: Verso Press, 1990; Lawrence Grossberg, Cary Nelson, and Paula Treichler, Eds., *Cultural Studies*. New York: Routledge, 1992; Sharon Welch, *A Feminist Ethic of Risk* (Minneapolis: Fortress Press, 1990); Iris Marion Young, *Justice and the Politics of Difference*. (Princeton: Princeton University Press, 1990); Stanley Aronowitz, *The Politics of Identity*. New York: Routledge, 1992); Jonathan Rutherford, Ed., *Identity, Community, Culture, Difference*. London: Lawrence and Wishart, 1990); Judith Butler, *Gender Trouble: Feminism and the Subversion of Identity*. New York: Routledge,1990); Russell Ferguson, Martha Gever, Trinh T. Minh-ha, and Cornel West, Eds., *Out There: Marginalization and Contemporary Cultures*. (Cambridge: MIT Press, 1990); Henry A. Giroux, *Border Crossings: Cultural Workers and the Politics of Education*. New York: Routledge, 1992).

20 Stuart Hall, "Cultural Identity and Diaspora," in Rutherford, Ed., op. cit., p. 226.

21 Rosalind Brunt, "The Politics of Identity." op. cit., p. 151.

22 This is clear not only in the way in which the popular press has launched a reductionistic attack on multiculturalism, cultural difference, and radical social

movements, but also in the mobilizing of conservative foundations and publishing houses to publish highly advertised books by leading neo-conservatives, who have made prosperous careers attacking the alleged "new McCarthyism" on the left. The examples are too numerous to cite but Dinesh D'Souza's *Illiberal Education* (New York: The Free Press, 1991) stands as a case.

23 Jonathan Rutherford, "A Place Called Home," op. cit., p. 11.

24 Rutherford, "A Place Called Home," op. cit., p. 11.

25 "Interview with Homi Bhabha," in Rutherford, Ed., op. cit., p. 208.

26 Homi K. Bhabha and Bhikhu Parekh, "Identities on Parade: A Conversation," *Marxism Today* (June 1989), pp. 2-5; Chandra Mohanty, "On Race and Voice: Challenges for Liberal Education in the 1990s," *Cultural Critique*, 14 (Winter 1989-1990), pp. 179-208).

27 Ellen Willis, "Multiple Identities," *Tikkun* Vol. 6, No. 6 (November-December, 1991), p. 58.

28 Jonathan Rutherford, "A Place Called Home," op. cit., p. 19.

29 Kobena Mercer, "Welcome to the Jungle: Identity and Diversity in Postmodern Politics," in Rutherford, Ed., op. cit, p. 44.

30 Jonathan Rutherford, "A Place Called Home," op. cot., p. 17.

31 One of the earliest attacks came from bell hooks. see bell hooks, *Ain't I a Woman*. Boston: South End Press, 1982.

32 Kobena Mercer, "Welcome to the Jungle," op. cit., p. 47.

33 Jonathan Rutherford, "A Place Called Home," op. cit., p. 17.

34 Pratibha Parmar, "Black Feminism: The Politics of Articulation," in Jonathan Rutherford, Ed., op. cit., 107.

35 Lawrence Grossberg, "The Context of Audience and the Politics of Difference," *Australian Journal of Communication*, No. 16 (1989), p. 106.

36 June Jordan interviewed in Pratibha Parmar, "Black Feminism: The Politics of Articulation," op. cit., p. 110.

37 Stuart Hall, "Cultural Identity and Diaspora," in Jonathan Rutherford, Ed., op. cit., p. 224.

38 Kobena Mercer, "Welcome to the Jungle," op. cit., p. 46.

39 Jeffrey Weeks, "The Value of Difference," in Jonathan Rutherford, Ed., op. cit., p. 98.

40 Stuart Hall, "Ethnicity: Identity and Difference," *Radical America*, Vol. 13, No. 4, (June 1991), pp. 15-16.

41 Homi Bhabha, "The Third Space," in Rutherford, Ed., op. cit., p. 211.

42 Homi Bhabha and Bhikhu Parekh, "Identities on Parade: A Conversation," *Marxism Today* (June 1989), p. 5.

43 Lemuel Johnson, "Caliban's Orientalism, Caliban's Occidentalism: (de)Generating Utopias." A talk delivered at the Minority Discourse Conference, Irvine, California, June 5, 1992.

44 The attempt to redefine the concept of the relationship between critical pedagogy and cultural work is also taken up in Henry A. Giroux, *Border Crossings: Cultural Workers and the Politics of Education* (New York: Routledge, 19992) and Roger I. Simon, *Teaching Against the Grain: A Pedagogy of Possibility* (New York: Bergin and Garvey Press, 1992).

45 This notion of pedagogy comes from: Roger Simon, *Teaching Against the Grain: A Pedagogy of Possibility* (New York: Bergin and Garvey, 1992).

46 Stuart Hall, "Ethnicity: Identity and Difference," *Radical America*, Vol. 13, No. 4 (June 1991), p. 10.

47 Nancy Fraser, "Rethinking the Public Sphere: A Contribution to the Critique of Actually Existing Democracy," *Social Text*, Nos. 25/26 (1990), p. 69.

4.

Living Dangerously

Identity Politics and the New Cultural Racism-
Towards a Critical Pedagogy of Representation

> The cult of ethnicity and its zealots have put at stake
> the American tradition of a shared commitment to
> common ideals and its reputation for assimilation, for
> making a 'nation' of nations. (Woodward, 1991, p.
> 43).

At the end of the 20th century, U.S. society is
becoming more racially and ethnically diverse; more
polarized along class lines; more alarmed by lesbians,
gay men, and other sexual minorities; more conscious
of gender differences; and, as a result, increasingly

preoccupied with political conflict over issues of representation. (Escoffier, 1991: 61)

Living Dangerously in
the Age of Identity Politics

As old borders and zones of cultural difference become more porous or eventually collapse, questions of culture increasingly become interlaced with the issues of power, representation, and identity. Dominant cultural traditions once self-confidently secure in the modernist discourse of progress, universalism, and objectivism are now interrogated as ideological beachheads used to police and contain subordinate groups, oppositional discourses, and dissenting social movements. Struggles over the academic canon, the conflict over multiculturalism, and the battle for either extending or containing the rights of new social groups dominate the current political and ideological landscape (Giroux, 1992). What is at stake in these struggles far exceeds the particular interests that structure any one of them or the specific terrains in which they are subject to debate, whether they be the academy, the arts, schools, or other spheres of public life. Underlying the proliferation of these diverse and various battles is a deeper conflict over the relationship between democracy and culture, on the one hand, and identity and the politics of representation on the other.

Central to this debate is an attempt to articulate the relationship among identity, culture and democracy in a new way. For the left, this has generally meant launching an assault on monumentalist views of Western culture, a one-dimensional Eurocentric academic canon, the autonomous subject as the sovereign source of truth, and forms of high culture which maintain sexist, racist, homophobic, and class specific relations of domination. More specifically, the challenges raised by feminism, postmodernism, and postcolonialism have contributed to a redefinition of cultural politics that addresses representational practices in terms that analyze not only their discursive power to construct common sense, textual authority, and particular social and racial formations, but also the "institutional conditions which regulate different fields of culture" (Bennett, 1992: 25). While many of the implications of such a cultural politics are still unclear, it has at the very least rendered visible, as Rita Felski (1989) points out, a number of important political/cultural projects. These include:

> the proliferation of information technologies and the gradual shift towards a postindustrial (although not postcapitalist) society, the declining authority of liberalism and Marxism as symptomatic of an increasing skepticism towards metanarratives, the reemergence of feminism and other social movements which have foregrounded difference and exposed the patriarchal, heterosexist, and ethnocentric nature of dominant Western ideals, an expanding aestheticization of every day life through the mass dissemination of signs and images and a simultaneous questioning of the art/life opposition inherent in high modernism, a shift in philosophical and social theory towards linguistic paradigms accompanied by a sustained critique of foundationalist thought. (Felski, 1989: 36).

The central challenge for educators and other cultural workers attempting to address these problems is to redefine the relationship between culture and politics in order to deepen and extend the basis for transformative and emancipatory practice. As part of a such a challenge, the political side of culture must be given primacy as an act of resistance and transformation by addressing issues of difference, identity, and textuality within rather than outside of the problematics of power, agency, and history. The urgent issue here is to link the politics of culture to the practice of a substantive democracy (Giroux, 1988). Stuart Hall and David Held (1990) foreground the importance of this task by arguing that any radical politics of representation and struggle must be situated within what they call "a contemporary politics of citizenship."

The value of such a politics is that it makes the complicated issue of difference fundamental to addressing the discourse of substantive citizenship; moreover, it favors looking at the conflict over relations of power, identity, and culture as central to a broader effort to advance the critical imperatives of a democratic society. Central to such a struggle is rethinking and rewriting difference in relation to wider questions of membership, community, and social responsibility.

A contemporary 'politics of citizenship' must take into account the role which the social movements have played in expanding the claims to rights and entitlements to new areas. [This means addressing] questions of membership posed by feminism, the black and ethnic movements, ecology and vulnerable minorities like children. But it must also come to terms with the problems posed by 'difference' in a deeper sense: for example, the diverse communities to which we belong, the complex interplay of identity and identification in modern society, and the differentiated ways in which people now participate in social life. The diversity of arenas in which citizenship is being claimed and contested today is essential to any modern conception of it because it is inscribed in the very logic of modern society itself (Hall and Held, 1990, p. 176).

Identity politics since the 1960s has played a significant role in refiguring a variety of human experiences within a discourse in which diverse political views, sexual orientations, races, ethnicities, and cultural differences are taken up in the struggle to construct counter-narratives and create new critical spaces and social practices.

Yet, the history of identity politics is not one that has moved unproblematically from resistance to a broader politics of democratic struggle. While identity politics was central to challenging the cultural homogeneity of the 1950s and providing spaces for marginal groups to assert the legacy and importance of their respective voices and experiences, it often failed to move beyond a notion of difference structured in polarizing binarisms and an uncritical appeal to a discourse of authenticity. Identity politics enabled many formerly silenced and displaced groups to emerge from the margins of power and dominant culture to reassert and reclaim suppressed identities and experiences; but in doing so, they often substituted one master narrative for another, invoked a politics of separatism, and suppressed differences within their own 'liberatory' narratives.

Despite the moralism, anti-intellectualism, and suspect romanticization of authentic experience associated with issues of identity politics, they have begun to occupy the center of academic and popular debates around concerns regarding culture, difference, and democratic renewal. Moreover, identity politics is no longer simply a one-dimensional, discursive feature of left wing theory and practice. At the same time, the radical possibilities associated with the link between democracy and the politics of cultural difference have not been lost on the New Right in the United States. In what has turned into a cultural blitz, the New Right of the Reagan/Bush era continuously chipped away at the legal, institutional, and ideological spheres necessary to the existence of a democratic society. During the last decade, conservatives have rolled back civil rights legislation, waged anti-pornography campaigns against the arts in order to eliminate public funding for 'politically offensive' groups, and attempted to replace state provision and public service with privatization programs designed to expand the power of capital, individual competitiveness, and corporate freedom (Giroux & Trend, 1992). One result has been the savaging of funds for public schools, health care programs, and an overall assault on the most basic presumptions of democratic life (Kozol, 1991).

Central to the new conservative offensive has been a renewed interest in addressing the radical politics that inform recent developments in the emerging discourses on culture and democracy. In particular, the New Right has focused on postmodernist, feminist, postcolonialist and other minority discourses that have raised serious questions regarding how particular forms of authority are secured through the organization of the curriculum at all levels of schooling. The radical call to reclaim the legacy of substantive democracy by reappropriating the language of equality, justice, and cultural difference have not been lost on conservative ideologues and public intellectuals. For example, Samuel Lipman (1989), writing in *The New Criterion*, argues that:

> culture and democracy cannot co-exist, for democracy by its nature represents the many, and culture, by its nature is created by the few. What the many cannot immediately comprehend, they destroy....What is necessary are definitions of culture and democracy based...less on inclusions and more on exclusions, less on finding similarities between conflicting realities, concepts, and goals and more on recognizing the differences between them. (pp. 15-16).

Lipman is not alone in viewing the extension of democratic ideology and political representation as a serious threat to dominant configurations of power and control. Conservative columnist and former presidential hopeful, Patrick Buchanan, openly embraces an authoritarian populism which views cultural democracy as a threat to the "American way of life." What is interesting for our purposes is the way in which Buchanan embraces the language of difference. For Buchanan, the reality of cultural difference, with its plurality of languages, experiences, and histories poses a serious threat to both national unity and what he defends as Judeo-Christian values. According to Buchanan, calls for expanding the existing limits of political representation and self-determination are fine as long as they allow Americans to 'take back' their country. In this conservative discourse, difference becomes a signifier for racial exclusivity, segregation, or in Buchanan's language, "self determination." For Buchanan, public life in the United States has deteriorated since 1965 because "a flood tide of immigration has rolled in from the Third World, legal and illegal, as our institutions of assimilation...disintegrated." Rewriting the discourse of nativism, Buchanan asks: "Who speaks for the Euro-Americans? Is it not time to take America back?" (quoted in Krauthammer, A-4). Similar comments were echoed by Buchannan in his speech at the Republican National Convention.

Similarly, right-wing Whites in America now echo a view of difference not as a marker for racial superiority but as a signifier for cultural containment, homogeneity, and social and structural inequality. The appeal is no longer to racial supremacy but to cultural uniformity parading under the politics of nationalism and patriotism. In this case, difference is removed from the language of biologism and firmly established as a cultural construct only to be reworked within a hegemonic project that connects race and nation against the elimination of structural and cultural inequality. In the same spirit of displaying difference in order to displace it within a hegemonic project of national unity, Frank Kermode, writing in *The New York Times*, dismisses some of the more articulate advocates of a progressive politics of difference as "a noisy crowd of antihomophobes, antiracists and antiwhites" (Kermode, 1992: 33). This is a remarkable statement that conjures up the specter of race as an ideological signpost for an assault on whites. Race in this context is invoked not to eliminate differences but to preserve them within self-contained cultural and social borders that prevent either crossing borders or forging new identities within new spaces or spheres of cultural difference. Of course, the Los Angeles uprising at the end of April 1992 not only ruptures the legitimacy of the new racial politics of containment, it also reveals how liberal and conservative discourses become complicitous with those underlying conditions that created the uprising by refusing to link race and class, by refusing to recognize that racism in the United States is deeply embedded in a politics of political economic and class divisions.

Renato Rosaldo (1989) focuses on the issue in arguing that "questions of culture seem to touch a nerve because they quickly become anguished questions of identity" (p. ix). The struggles emerging over "anguished questions of identity" have taken a new turn in the last decade. The "culture wars" that have beset American politics since the advent of the Reagan/Bush reign have become increasingly dominated by a politics of representation rooted in an authoritarian populist discourse that is powerfully refiguring the relationship between identity and culture, particularly as it is addressed in the discourse of racial difference.

There is a certain irony in the fact that at this current historical conjuncture, when many leftist critics appear to be fed up with identity politics, conservatives have seized upon it with a vengeance.[1] Writing in *Tikkun* Magazine, leftist social critic, Ilene Philipson reduces identity politics to the discourse of anxiety, alienation, and inadequacy. In this view, attempts on the part of various social groups to combat racism, homophobia, or sexism are overly determined by psychological concerns over self-identity, self esteem, and anomie. Philipson makes the point succinctly:

> Identity politics provides a way of avoiding self-blame
> for feelings of powerlessness and anomie that are, at
> their root, politically and socially constructed. But as
> such, the politics of identity inevitably misdirects our
> attention away from the fact that, apart from a tiny
> group at the top of the class hierarchy (to use a
> forgotten term), alienation, a sense of not being
> recognized for who one is, and feelings of impotence
> and failure affect us all-certainly to different degrees
> and with different repercussions....identity politics is
> not sufficiently radical to speak to this distress, to get
> at the root sources of our alienation and individually
> experienced lack of social recognition.(1991:54)

Philipson's reductionism is disturbing. Identity politics covers a complex and diverse terrain of theoretical positions and discourses concerned with questions of subjectivity, culture, difference, and struggle. In its hard and soft versions, this terrain extends from the cultural politics of black nationalists like Louis Farrakhan to the more radically progressive discourses of ethnicity and cultural difference in the works of Stuart Hall and Homi K. Bhabha. But there is more at stake here than a species of theoretical carelessness on the part of left critics who simply dismiss identity politics as separatist, elitist, and reactionary, there is also the politically shortsighted willingness to abandon identity politics at a time when right wing conservatives are reappropriating progressive critiques of race, ethnicity, and identity and using them to promote rather than dispel a politics of cultural racism. This is a serious mistake. While the end of identity politics is something that left critics and cultural workers seem to be endlessly debating, they do not appear to have fully come to grips with its political and racial consequences. As Stuart Clarke (1991) points out, the issue of identity politics will not go away in the 1990s. Identity politics has become one of the more powerful common sense constructions developed by the right wing in its attempt to "blunt progressive political possibilities...[by privileging] race as a sign of social disorder and civic decay" (Clarke, 1991: 37).

Rather than merely dismissing identity politics, leftist cultural workers need to engage the issue more dialectically. In this case, a critical perspective on identity politics should be seen as fundamental to any discourse and social movement that believes in the radical renewal of democratic society. With this qualification in mind, the relationship between identity and politics can be reformulated within a politics of representation which is open to contingency, difference, and self-reflexivity but still able to engage in an emancipatory project that reconstructs public life through a politics of democratic solidarity. Not to do so is to place left social movements and cultural workers outside rather than inside of the public debate about identity, difference, and culture. Stuart Clarke puts it well: "The point of this is to indicate that the complex, even contradictory, character of identity politics must be accounted for in efforts to develop a politically effective critical perspective. Identity politics will remain a persistent feature of our political landscape in part because it produces limited but real empowerment for its participants" (1991: 46).

In part, Clarke's concern is legitimated by the ideological shift that has taken place among cultural conservatives in the last few years. With the advent of the assault by a wide range of conservative groups on "political correctness," multiculturalism, and radical intellectuals in the academy, identity politics has replaced the Cold War signifier of "communism" as the most serious domestic threat to the New World Order.[2] Moreover, in response to this threat, pedagogy and the issue of cultural representation have become strategic forces used by the New Right and other conservative groups in mobilizing an authoritarian populist movement. Three important issues are at stake here. First, the New Right has developed a powerful new strategy for abstracting cultural difference from the discourse of democracy and social justice. Central to such a discourse is the attempt to fuse culture within a tidy formation that equates the nation, citizenship, and patriotism with a racially exclusive notion of difference. Second, it is crucial to recognize that conservatives have given enormous prominence to waging a cultural struggle over the control and use of the popular media and other spheres of representation in order to "articulate contemporary racial meanings and identities in new ways, to link race with more comprehensive political and cultural agendas, to interpret social structural phenomena (such as inequality or social policy) with regard to race" (Winant, 1990: 125). Third, it is imperative that the left not only construct a new politics of difference but extend and deepen the possibilities of critical cultural work by reasserting the primacy of the pedagogical as a form of cultural politics.

In what follows, I will analyze more specifically the ideological contours of the old and new politics of difference. I will then analyze how the some of the basic assumptions of the new politics of difference are used in the film, *Grand Canyon*, to refigure dominant social and racial identities. I will conclude by considering the implications the above discussion has for a critical pedagogy of representation. In doing so, I will stress the importance of reworking the relationship between cultural workers and pedagogy as part of a broader politics of representation, political practice, and emancipatory change.

Representation, Difference, and the New Politics of Race

The culturalism of the new racism has gone hand in hand with a definition of race as a matter of difference rather than a question of hierarchy. In another context Fanon refers to a similar shift as a progression from vulgar to cultural racism....Culture is conceived along ethnically absolute lines, not as something intrinsically

fluid, changing, unstable, and dynamic, but as a fixed
property of social groups rather than a relational field
in which they encounter one another and live out
social, historical relationships. When culture is brought
into contact with race it is transformed into a
pseudobiological property of communal life. (Gilroy,
1990: 266)

The old racism developed within the historical legacy of
colonialism and modern slavery and rested on a blatant ideological
appeal to pseudo-biological and scientific theories of racism to justify
inequality, hierarchies and exploitation as part of the universal order.
In this racism, the Other's identity warrants its very annihilation
because it is seen as impure, evil, and inferior. Moreover, whiteness
represents itself as a universal marker for being civilized and in doing
so posits the Other within the language of pathology, fear, madness,
and degeneration (Gilman, 1985).

Within dominant regimes of representation, the old racism
trades in classic stereotypes, grounds Otherness in fixed, trans-
historical and cultural categories, and refuses to address the structural
and ideological foundations of racist cultural practices (Goldberg,
1990). Racist ideology in this case collapses the meaning of being the
Other into the representation of Otherness.[3] In its various forms, there
is little effort to make inequality, racism, or powerlessness
problematic, open to discussion, in other words, this is a racism that
refuses to critically engage in ethical and political terms its own
privileged site of enunciation. It is the racism of *The Birth of a Nation*,
the black exploitation films of the 1960s, the school textbooks filled
with grotesque stereotypes of blacks. It is a racist practice that offers
no apologies and focuses on how one inhabits dominant
representations/beliefs rather than on the beliefs themselves as the basis
for constructing common sense. In the words of Stuart Hall (1988),
the old racism is organized through the epistemic discourse of the
violence of the Other. Based on fear and desire, the old racism
attempts to construct blacks as the object rather the subject of
representation, a process that allows whiteness to remain unproblematic

even as it projects onto the black subject its own fantasies of noble primitiveness and reckless violence. The old racism "operates by constructing impassable symbolic boundaries between racially constituted categories, and its typically binary system of representation constantly marks and attempts to fix and naturalize the difference between belongingness and Otherness" (Hall, 1988: 28).

We are now witnessing in the United States (and in Europe) the emergence of a new racism and politics of cultural difference expressed both in the reconfiguration of the relationship between Otherness and difference, on the one hand, and meaning and the politics of representation on the other (Winant, 1990; Policar, 1990; Taguieff, 1990; Clarke, 1991)) . Underlying the emergence of the new politics of racism and difference is a deep ambivalence on the part of liberals and conservatives about the traditional categories that have been used to defend racist practices. Identifications grounded in the racial superiority of whites, the fixing of Anglo-European culture as synonymous with civilization itself, and the civilizing mission of patriarchal, Eurocentric discourse are no longer easily maintained within mainstream ideologies and regimes of representation. The new social movements of the 1960s, the reception of feminist, postmodernist, and postcolonialist discourses in the 1970s, the development of critical popular cultural forms in the 1980s, and the rise of the new ethnicities with their challenge to liberal pluralism in the 1990s, have necessitated a new politics of difference and representation of racial politics on the part of both the left and the New Right (West, 1990). As American life becomes more hybridized, the distinctions between in what Emily Hicks (1991) calls "original and alien cultures" have become more difficult to maintain theoretically and politically. As new cultural boundaries and spaces emerge crisscrossed with a diversity of Otherness, dominant strategies of representation are abrogated and struggled over through an ongoing process of negotiation, translation, and transformation. The sensibility that informs the relationship between cultural borders reorders the codes of reference for engaging cultural differences and their related networks of hierarchy, power, and struggle.

With these qualifications in mind, any analysis of the new cultural politics of difference and race must acknowledge the shift in the "dominant regimes of representation" (Hall, 1988) around race and multiculturalism that has occurred in the national and popular press within the last few years. In theoretical terms, this points to a proliferation of competing discourses that not only challenges the old vocabulary on race but also expands the sites from which notions of whiteness and blackness, among others, are made visible, rewritten, and circulated. At the same, since there is no longer any single articulating principle defining the racial dimensions of cultural work and life, the audiences which are the subject and object of racial enunciations have become more complex, contradictory, and multilayered. On one level this has led to what Stuart Hall (1988, 1991) calls the end of the innocent black subject. At stake here is the recognition that "'black' is essentially a politically- and culturally-constructed category, which cannot be grounded in a set of fixed trans-cultural or transcendental racial categories and which therefore has no guarantees in Nature" (Hall, 1988: p. 28). Hence, issues of being black are abstracted from the language of essentialism and scientism and shifted to the terrain of representation. As Hall puts it, "The end of the essential black subject...entails a recognition that the central issues of race always appear historically in articulation, in a formation, with other categories and divisions and are constantly crossed and recrossed by the categories of class, of gender, and ethnicity" (1988: 28).

Within this discourse the relationship between identity and being "black" is no longer fixed, static, or secure. Hall's position offers cultural workers new opportunities to rewrite the politics of representation around race and difference by deconstructing in historical and relational terms not only the central categories of "Otherness," but also the dominant, discourses and representations that secure "whiteness" as a universalizing norm (Young, 1990; Dyer, 1988; hooks, 1990). At stake here is the need to create a new political vocabulary and project for rethinking a politics of cultural difference predicated on broader conceptions of race and identity. In this case, cultural workers need to construct a notion of border identity that challenges any essentialized notion of subjectivity while simultaneously demonstrating that the self as a historical and cultural formation is shaped in complex, related, and multiple ways through their interaction with numerous and diverse communities (Fraser, 1992). Needless to say, such a project has posed and continues to pose a serious threat to the hegemonic politics of race and representation practiced by conservatives. The challenge has not been lost on the New Right.

Whereas the Bush era began with the image of Willie Horton and the implication that black criminality offered the principal signifier to underscore the cultural concerns of racism, the new cultural racism has shifted the emphasis from a notion of difference equated with deviance and cultural deprivation to a position that acknowledges racial diversity only to proclaim that different racial formations, ethnicities, and cultures pose a threat to national unity. Racial privilege is no longer maintained primarily through the use of terror or other traditional neofascist techniques. The struggle for racial privilege based on an implicit model of white supremacy or cultural nationalism takes many forms among conservatives and right wing liberals, but underlying all of these efforts is an attempt to "rearticulate racial meanings, to reinterpret the content of 'whiteness' and the politics that flows from it" (Winant, 1990: 126). One instance of this hegemonic project is a politics of representation that suggests that whites are the victims of racial inequality. In this discourse the social gravity of poverty, economic exploitation, and class divisions are removed from any analysis of race. The strategy for such a politics gathered a powerful momentum during the Reagan era with the practice of "coding" racial meanings so as to mobilize white fears. Hence, the use of terms such as quotas, busing, welfare, and multiculturalism as signifiers to arouse the insecurities and anger of whites. Another instance of the new politics of racism is expressed in displaying racial difference as a significant aspect of American life, but doing so only to pose it as a threat that has to be overcome. This strategy became particularly clear in the aftermath of the Los Angeles uprising. The dominant press repeatedly labeled the uprising as a riot, and consistently referred to the events that took place as acts of lawlessness. In this case, the politics of the new racism revealed itself shamelessly in the Bush Administration's efforts to respond to the L.A.

uprising by claiming that it was caused by the failed liberal social programs inaugurated by President Lyndon Johnson in the 1960s. What is really under assault here are not the social, economic, and political conditions that made the uprising possible, but the Voting Rights Act of 1965, and various programs that launched Aid to Families with Dependent Children, Head Start, Chapter 1, Food Stamps, and other public reform efforts. The most disgraceful response to the uprising, one which fully embodied the sentiments of the new racism, came from the *National Review*, which claimed that the main lesson of the insurrections was that law abiding people (read whites) need more police to protect themselves, and that the real cause of the uprising was "bitterness nursed by many blacks [which] is largely the bequest of people like Reverend Jackson and Representative Waters, who have a stake in fermenting divisive race-consciousness"(Johnson, 1992, p. 17).

Surprisingly, these two strategies are not fundamentally at odds with each other. In the first instance, conservatives invoke racial separation in order to mobilize white fears and to organize a constituency for implementing mainstream policy initiatives. In the second instance, racial difference is attacked as something to be overcome. In this discourse, whiteness as a signifier of power and privilege becomes the unspoken referent for naming and passing judgment on the continuing efforts of radicals, minorities, and others to organize around racial and class differences in pressing for political, educational, cultural, and social reforms. Evoking the racially-coded language and images of national unity, conservative groups have attempted to dismantle the progressive elements of racial politics by advocating standardized testing in the public schools, attacking multiculturalism as a threat to a "common culture," and deploying cultural pluralism as slogan which displays difference without mentioning dominant relations of power and class oppression. Winant (1990) argues that the new racial politics of the New Right and Neoconservativism articulate with a wider cultural and political agenda that resists any policy which threatens "the fundamentally integrative, if not assimilationist, character of the 'American ethnic pattern', market rationality, anti-statism, the merits of individualism, and respect for the 'high culture' of the West" (Winant, 1990: 132).

In what follows, I want to analyze the film *Grand Canyon* first in order to illustrate how the new politics of difference and race is being constructed within a Hollywood version of identity politics. This analysis is intended to examine how a representational politics actively marks its subjects through racially coded forms of address and enunciation in which subject positions are made available and desires mobilized and where "spectacles of identity politics interact with the construction of common sense"(Clarke, 1991: 47). In the last section of this chapter, I will develop some central elements of a pedagogy of representation that offers possibilities for developing an educational practice of decolonization in which the act of representing can be addressed historically and semiotically as a part of an emancipatory attempt to situate relations between the self and others within a broader struggle for a more just and democratic society.

New Age Whiteness and the Politics of Difference

> America's sense of its own 'radical innocence' has its most profound origins in [the] belief that there is a basic humanity unaltered by the diversity of the citizens who share in it. Democracy is the universal quantifier by which America, the 'melting pot', the 'nation of immigrants,' constitutes itself as a nation. If *all* our citizens can be said to be Americans, this is not because we share any positive characteristics, but rather because we have all been given the right to shed these characteristics, to present ourselves as disembodied before the law. I divest myself of positive identity, therefore I am a citizen. (Copjec, 1991: 30)

As we move into an age in which cultural space becomes unfixed, unsettled, porous, and hybrid, it becomes increasingly difficult either to defend notions of singular identity or to deny that different groups, communities, and people are increasingly bound to

each other in a myriad of complex relationships. Modes of
representation that legitimized a world of strict cultural separation,
collective identities, and rigid boundaries seem hopelessly outdated as
the urban landscape is being rewritten within new and shifting borders
of identity, race, and ethnicity. New cultural spaces, borderlands,
identities, texts, and crossings have created something of a panic
among those groups who control dominant regimes of representation.
Whereas in the past, the response to racial inequality was to pretend it
didn't exist, the current reaction is to re-present it without changing the
social, economic, and political conditions that create it. Indifference
and silence, or even worse, an appeal to outright racist supremacy,
have reluctantly given way to forms of negotiation and translation as
varied ethnicities, races, and cultural differences assert themselves both
within and between diverse communities. Dominant society no longer
resorts to exterminating or silencing Others; nor can they simply erase
them. Cultural difference has descended on America like the fog.
Dominant groups are now driving very carefully through a cultural
terrain in which whiteness can no longer remain invisible as a racial,
political, and historical construction. The privilege and practices of
domination that underscore being white in America can no longer
remain invisible through either an appeal to a universal norm or a
refusal to explore how whiteness works to produce a forms of
"friendly" colonialism.[4]

Los Angeles seems to exemplify the changing nature of the
metropolitan urban terrain and the cultural politics that appear to
besiege it.[5] The hybridized cultural landscape of Los Angeles has
been mythologized in Dennis Hopper's depiction of gang life in
Colors, rendered as a borderland where cyborgs and humans rewrite
the meaning of identity and difference in Ridley Scott's *Bladerunner*
and brilliantly taken up through the complex relations that constitute
the coming of age experiences of mostly black young men in a
neighborhood in South Central Los Angeles in John Singleton's *Boyz N*
the Hood. In all of these films, Los Angeles is portrayed against a
gritty reality in which cultural differences produce a borderland where
an apocalyptic vision of the future is played out amid growing forms of
daily violence, resistance, fear, and struggle. Difference in these films

is neither innocent nor removed from wider social and political articulations.

In *Grand Canyon*, directed by Lawrence Kasdan, Los Angeles once again becomes a prophetic site for understanding how the language and relations of cultural differences are reshaping public culture in the happy boutique neighborhoods of the rich and the privileged. As in the films mentioned above, Los Angeles becomes an important signifier in order to comment about fear, violence, and racial politics as they are rewritten within the changing understanding of Otherness and the growing self consciousness of what it means to be white in America. What is interesting about *Grand Canyon* is that it goes beyond the empty pluralism that always racializes the Other but never makes whiteness visible. In fact, Kasdan presents a narrative in which whiteness becomes the major referent for defining and acknowledging the responsibility that whites have in a world in which they define themselves as racially and culturally under siege.

Grand Canyon embodies the reactionary side of identity politics, but it does not echo the shrill fanaticism of a Pat Buchanan, Jesse Helms, or Pat Robertson. Instead, it mobilizes those fears and desires of white folks who recognize that cultural differences are here to stay, but don't want to be positioned so as to call their own racism or complicity with economic, social, and political inequalities into question. The central white characters in Kasdan's film want to exercise good conscience, retain their property values, and still be able to jog without being mugged. Their racism is more subtle, clean, and New Age. Racial Otherness represents a pragmatic rather than an ethical dilemma for them. Border crossings become an excuse for acknowledging the collapse of public life without having to take responsibility for it.

Kasdan's *Grand Canyon* attempts to erase the problem and politics of representation by refusing to portray the complexity of social, political and cultural forces that structure relationships between whites and blacks, on the one hand, and men and women on the other. But it is important to note, particularly with regard to white/black relations, that Kasdan does not rely on traditional modes of representation. That is, he does not resort to addressing the issue of cultural difference by simply including the Other in the script. He does not attempt to secure filmic legitimacy simply by covering the story and including the requisite number of blacks. On the contrary, Kasdan is more vigilant and intent on rewriting and re-imaging how Otherness is presented in ways that don't "permit or make for interventions on the part of those (Others) represented" (Mariani and Crary, 1990: 97). In this case, Kasdan's view of racial conflict, poverty, sexism, and public life are defined within a monolithic notion of whiteness which fails to question the place of white racism as a historical and social construction. Consequently, Kasdan provides a celluloid mapping of racial conflict and cultural differences that are resolved in a dystopian politics that subordinates human agency to the grand forces of nature and allows whites to feel good about themselves while simultaneously resolving them of any responsibility in either constructing or maintaining those ideological and structural forces that privilege agency for some groups and greatly limit it for others. Goodwill and choice combine in this film to create a New Age sense of possibility which in the final analysis collapses irreducible differences among blacks, whites, and women into the airy recognition that we are all secondary to the larger natural forces of good and evil that shape the planet and thus provide a common ground on which to recognize how goodness can flow out of despair, how agency is limited by nature, and how ethics is powerless against nature's unfolding. What is missed in Kasdan's New Age ideology, as Michael Dyson (1991) points out in a different context, is "how choice itself is not a property of autonomous moral agents acting in an existential vacuum, but rather something that is created and exercised within the interaction of social, psychic, political, and economic forces of everyday experiences"(p. 75). Of course, it could be argued since Kasdan refuses in *Grand Canyon* to disrupt the ideological, textual, and structural codes that inform race relations in this country, his approach simply reflects the traditional colonial policy of reinscribing potentially disruptive social relations in order to contain them. But where Kasdan takes a different theoretical and political twist is in his attempt to produce forms of cultural self-representation in which whites are simultaneously portrayed as both the victims of cultural change and the only gatekeepers of a society which appears to be on the verge of self destruction. In this form of cultural representation, radical innocence becomes the signifier for a hegemonic practice that colonizes the normal through a notion of common sense in which race, inequality, and power are eventually erased in a New Age vision of goodwill where luck and chance rather than struggle and agency police the present and predict the future. Though willing to admit that the landscape of cultural difference has radically changed in America in the last twenty years, Kasdan presents his audiences with a hegemonic notion of cultural "innocence" in which it is argued that there "still exists a precious, universal, 'innocent' instance in which we can all recognize ourselves" (Copjec, 1991: 30).

Encounters With Otherness

> Historically-speaking, every community has felt forced to accept change, to at least come to terms with other communities. The question is, when do communities become frozen? When do they say that they will not change any more? I think that happens when they feel besieged, threatened, when no space is left for them to grow (Bhabha and Parekh, 1989: 4).

Grand Canyon is most importantly about whites becoming self conscious of race and otherness as central determinants in shaping the existing social, political, and cultural landscape, but also in providing a referent for a new politics and form of ethical address. This referent combines for whites the opportunity to acknowledge this new landscape without having to give up their power or privilege. At the heart of the story is an attempt to define what being white, male, and privileged means when the encounter with the harsh colonial terrain of American society can no longer be avoided by the rich and the powerful. *Grand Canyon* attempts to mediate the traditional white phobia of race mixing through the liberal assertion of the right to be different. Couched in the discourse of pluralism, this particular notion of cultural difference presents whiteness "more as a case of historical accident, rather than a characteristic cultural/historical construction, achieved through white domination" (Dyer, 1988: 46). Whiteness as a category is rendered invisible as a symbol of ethnicity, while simultaneously avowed as a major category to normalize definitions of class, race, gender, heterosexuality, and nationality (Llyod, 1992). Similarly, *Grand Canyon* does not address cultural differences by acknowledging the wider grid of social relations marked by existing systems of inequality and discrimination. Hence, there is no sense in this film of how "different groups are related to each other within networks of hierarchy and exploitation"(Welch, 1989: 128). Understood in these terms, the film attempts first to renegotiate the possibilities for whites to acknowledge those Others who have been marginalized in American society less as human beings caught in the vice of oppression and exploitation than as a threat to unitary sense of white identity and national unity. Second, *Grand Canyon* attempts to develop an articulation between unity and difference that reinforces whiteness as a discourse, referent, and practice of power. Third, the film uses racism as the basis for white self criticism but in doing so is silent about the mutuality of responsibility between whites and blacks in addressing issues of ethnicity and social change. These points can be more fully developed by analyzing how the overarching narrative that structures *Grand Canyon* is organized around three different sets of relations: the social divisions between whites and blacks; the relationship between men and women; and the relationship between human beings and nature.

Black and white relationships are primarily developed between the encounter that Mack (Kevin Kline), a wealthy immigration lawyer, has with Simon (Danny Glover), a mechanic who virtually saves Mack from being assaulted by a black gang after he gets lost while driving home from a Lakers basketball game. The context of the meeting is central to the relationship.

In order to avoid heavy traffic after the game, Mack tries taking a shortcut and drives into a black neighborhood that immediately appears to be both alien and menacing. Difference looms up before Mack as strange, unfamiliar, and ominous. As Mack drives along the streets of the neighborhood with its boarded-up houses, numerous liquor stores, and mix of homeless, poor, and roaming youth, he hears the sound of rap music exploding all around him. A car drives by filled with four black youths who wave menacingly to him. Suddenly, his new Lexus dies and he is trapped in a zone of difference coded with racial fear and danger. He uses his car phone to call for a tow truck, but the phone stops working and he is forced to leave the safety of his Lexus and use a public phone. His fear at this point rises to the point of desperation. He tells the tow truck dispatcher that if a driver doesn't show up soon he may lose his life and not just his car. His fear has reached the point of desperation, and he races back to his car to wait for the tow-truck. Within minutes, the car playing the rap music, surely a signifier of danger to the yuppie lawyer, pulls up behind Mack's Lexus. Four young men get out of the car and begin to taunt him. Clearly, Mack's life is in danger. One of the young men has a gun tucked in his belt and gestures to it while telling Mack to get out of the car. Mack gets out and tells them they can have what ever they want. The young man snarls at him. The binarism between Mack as the model of decency and the young black men as a threatening symbol of social savagery skillfully works to portray whites as a besieged group while simultaneously portraying inner city black youths as a signifier of danger and social decay.

Chance and danger, another major subtext of the film, emerges when Simon, the black tow truck driver arrives on the scene. Exhibiting street wise savvy and courage, Simon convinces the young men to cool out and go back to roaming the streets. Simon is the model of the cool, tough, yet responsible, black man. He lives alone. Not only does he support a deaf daughter who attends a college in Washington, D. C., he also helps support his sister, who lives with a son who is gradually being lost to the L. A. black gang culture. Simon's life is complicated. Trapped within the limits imposed by poverty, racism, and the culture of survival, Simon maintains a view of society that allows him to go on with his life but undercuts his own sense of individual and collective agency.

Sitting with Mack while the Lexus is being repaired, Simon tells him that he once visited the Grand Canyon. He recalls how it made him realize how insignificant life is in the long haul. For Simon, the message is clear: humans within the larger scheme of nature are minute and transitory. Humbled before the long duration of history and time that inscribes the vastness and wonder of the Grand Canyon, Simon substitutes a New Age naturalism for a notion of critical agency and social possibility.

Mack is so grateful to Simon for saving his car and life that he later takes him out to breakfast, develops a friendship with him, and in doing so crosses over a racial boundary that allows him to recognize difference as part of daily life but at the same time he refrains from questioning his own place in the larger economy of power and privilege that largely relegates blacks to a subaltern status in contemporary American society.

The relationship between Simon and Mack is mutually reinforced through their sense that the world is organized through a random sense of chance, luck, and danger. For Mack, this is an important insight that allows him to assuage his liberal conscience by helping Simon's sister find an apartment in a safer neighborhood, and fixing Simon up with a black women who works for Mack's law firm. In this context, Mack's whiteness is not understood through the evocation of a critical reading of history, an invocation of dangerous memory, or an understanding of how social relations that evoke privileges and power must be unlearned and transformed. On the contrary, whiteness for Mack becomes a referent for self-sacrifice buttressed by the liberal assumption that as a privileged white man he can solve the problems of marginalized and subordinate Others. For Simon, Mack exemplifies how history turns merely on luck and circumstance. After all, what are the chances of an inner-city, black mechanic either meeting or becoming friends with a high-powered, privileged, yuppie white lawyer. Simon displays his gratitude to Mack at the end of the film by driving his sister and her young boy along with Mack and his family to the Grand Canyon. It is here in the face of the wonder of nature that the immensity of the racial, cultural, political, economic, and social differences that separate these families are erased in a New Age notion of unity and spirituality.

The relationship between whites and blacks/Others is also revealed through the coming of age narrative of two young men in the film. Mack and Claire's son, named after Roberto Clemente, the famous Puerto Rican baseball player, is portrayed in terms that suggest he leads a relatively untroubled life. Roberto is from a rich family, goes to a decent school, develops a romance with a young woman in summer camp, and appears to be on his way to a successful future. The most serious tension in his life appears to be learning how to drive and coping with a name that contradicts his own refusal to view himself as ethnic. Learning how to make a left turn in traffic appears to be the most pressing test he will face in the near future.

On the other hand, Simon's nephew is portrayed as a black young male who has given his life up to the L.A. gang culture. The source of this black teenage boy's problems comes from living with a single parent who cannot contain him and residing in a community filled with crime and despair over which he has no control. Kasdan presents the film audience with a view of black urban life that is as one dimensional as the stereotypes and tropes he uses to construct the coming-of-age odyssey of a black youth growing up in a poor, inner-city neighborhood. The suffocating conditions of urban decay, rampant poverty, and random violence are frozen by Kasdan in a series of images that refuse to analyze those historical, cultural, economic, and political conditions that provide some dialectical grounding for understanding how domination, power, resistance, and identity come together to reveal the complexity of life in such a setting. The binarism created by Kasdan of growing up 'black' and 'white' does not suggest what these two young men share in common, how one form of life relates to the other, or how new identities might be constructed by transforming these related sites of privilege and oppression. In this scenario, whiteness is not only privileged, it is also the only referent for social change, hope, and action. Within the rigid binarism portraying these two very different coming-of-age experiences cast in racial terms, blacks are equated with lawlessness while whites are seen as a paragon of rationality, compassion, and stability. Once again, what is revealed here is a fundamental disrespect for marginalized Others manifest in the refusal to analyze what whiteness as a category of power means (or suggests) in terms of its ethical relations with Others. This type of disrespect for the Other is also manifested throughout the film in the refusal to allow those who are oppressed, blacks, women, and children to speak for themselves, to be the subject of resistance and historical agency, and to be complexly represented within rather than outside of the specificity of their daily lives.

Otherness as both a marker of deficit and a resource to redefine whiteness as a universal symbol of unity and hope is displayed in a number of other relations throughout the film. Race and gender intersect in a dominating fashion through the portrayal of Mack's wife, Claire (Mary MacDonnell). Caught in a mid-life crisis, Claire appears to solve her problem while taking her daily jog. Passing the nearby woods, she finds an abandoned third world baby. Ignoring the concrete identity of the child (Why was she abandoned? What history, memories, and pain inform this act? What does such an act suggest about the ethical relations between the wealthy and the poor in terms of their respective problems, hopes, and plans for the future?) Kasdan uses this intersection of "chance and luck" to suggest that Claire's identity is entirely dependent on her providing nurturance to Others, particularly since she can no longer provide such nurturance to her husband and teenage son. Claire eventually adopts the baby and in doing so not only secures her own identity but also affirms the notion of self-sacrifice, guilt, and duty that appears to be endemic to Kasdan's conception of how responsible action is constituted for whites. A subtext of this relationship is that third world families are not responsible enough to raise their own children. Conversely, in this case, colonialism is seen as having its benefits.

Claire is not much different than all of the women who inhabit the celluloid landscape of Grand Canyon. Mack's mistress, Simon's lover, and Claire are women whose identities are largely shaped in the image of men. Kasdan suggests that their only desires are rooted in the patriarchal demands for women (not men) to nurture, raise children, or find a "good" man. Deprived of a complex identity and voice, all of the women in this film lack any sense of agency or the need to redefine their lives outside of the imperatives of a patriarchal culture. Moreover, Kasdan also uses a debilitating binarism in framing the differences among the women in Grand Canyon. Either they are viewed as little more than prostitutes, as is the case with Kline's mistress, Dee (Mary-Louise Parker), or they are viewed as selfless saints, an image embodied in Claire (who is viewed in a number of scenes through the figure of the madonna rocking the baby Jesus).

Finally, all of the main characters in this film share the belief that some miraculous force establishes connections between people who inhabit the planet and that this force expresses itself through the circumstances of luck, chance, and fate. Mack tells Simon, for instance, that he believes that God once appeared to him in the form of a woman wearing a baseball cap and saved him from being hit by a bus. Clearly, his time to die had not come. Simon reveals his own infatuation with nature and the insignificance of human life and agency in the face of the wonder and awe of the Grand Canyon. Claire believes that finding the baby was orchestrated by some higher force. Thus, she doesn't have to bother with the social, political, and ideological consequences of either the abandonment of a third world child or her adopting a baby under such circumstances. In the end, the primacy of the social, political, and cultural as they are manifested in various problems informing cultural differences, gender issues, and the problematic of ethnicity are wiped away in a New Age adoration of the mysteries and wonders of nature. All of life's riddles are seemingly resolved when all the central players end up in the final scene of the film staring with amazement and awe at the aesthetic wonder of the Grand Canyon. Clearly, in this scenario, nature and social Darwinism are on the side of white domination as all of the differences that brought together these various men, women, and children are removed from the systemic injustices which influence their respective lives. History, power, and agency now dissolve into the abyss of liberal goodwill, New Age uplift thinking, and a dead-end pastoralism. Cultural differences dissolve into a regime of representations that universalize harmonizing systems while eliminating the discourse of power, conflict, and struggle.

Toward a Pedagogy of Representation and Representational Pedagogy

The question I want to take up here is how cultural workers might extend and deepen the politics of representation by addressing what I call a critical pedagogy of representation and a representational pedagogy. In the first instance, I am referring to the various ways in which representations are constructed as a means of comprehending the past through the present in order to legitimate and secure a particular view of the future. How students can come to interrogate the historical, semiotic and relational dynamics involved in the production of various regimes of representations and their respective politics. In other words, a pedagogy of representation focuses on demystifying the act and process of representing by revealing how meanings are produced within relations of power that narrate identities through history, social forms, and modes of ethical address that appear objective, universally valid and consensual. At issue here is the task of both identifying how representational politics work to secure dominant modes of authority and mobilize popular support while also interrogating how the act of presenting is developed within forms of textual authority and relations of power "which always involve choice, selectivity, exclusions, and inclusions" (Said in Mariani and Crary, 1990: 96).

Central to a pedagogy of representation is the need to provide students with the opportunities to deconstruct the mythic notion that images, sounds, and texts merely express reality. More specifically, a critical pedagogy of representation recognizes that students inhabit a photocentric, aural, and televisual culture in which the proliferation of photographic and electronically produced images and sounds serve to actively produce knowledge and identities within particular sets of ideological and social practices (Simon, 1992). By granting the concept of representation a formative and not merely an expressive place in the constitution of social and political life, questions of subjectivity, power, and politics take on an increasing significance as a pedagogical practice in which the relationship between difference and identity must be located within rather than outside of the mediations of history, culture, and ideology (Giroux and McLaren in Schwoch, White, Reily, 1992). On one level, this suggests that students must analyze those institutions that constantly work through the power of representations and social practices to "produce, codify, and even rewrite histories of race and colonialism in the name of difference" (Mohanty, 1989/90: 184). Representations are not simply forms of cultural capital necessary for human beings to present themselves in relation to others and human nature, they also inhabit and sustain institutional structures that need to be understood and analyzed within circuits of power that constitute what might be called a political economy of representations. In this case, a pedagogy and politics of representation would highlight historically how "machineries of representation" within the growth of new mass communication and information technologies are inextricably linked to the emergence of corporate-controlled and knowledge-based societies in which a politics of representation must be partly understood within the imperatives of the newly emerging transnational market economies of the postmodern age (Schiller, 1986, 1989; Schneider and Wallis, 1988; Tomilinson, 1991;). This insight has provoked Trinh T. Minh-ha to remark:

> to address the question of production relations...is endlessly to reopen the question: how is the real (or the social ideal of good representation) produced? Rather than catering to it, striving to capture and discover its truth as a concealed or lost object, it is therefore important also to keep asking: How is truth being ruled? (1990: 85)

In part, Stuart Hall (1988) further extends this insight in arguing that cultural workers must address not only the relations of representations, how their machineries work to actively produce common sense notions of identity and difference, but also how dominant regimes of representation actively "structure conditions of existence...outside of the sphere of the discursive" (p. 27). By providing students with critical tools to decode dominating machineries of representation, their own locations and social formations can be understood in terms that allow them to introduce into their discourse "a sense of the political which ultimately leads to a consideration of power" (Borsa, 1990:31).

Drawing on the work of Abigail Solomon-Godeau (1991), I want to argue that there are three principle elements at work in a pedagogy of representation. First, cultural workers must identify the historically contingent nature of the form and content of a particular form of representation. In the case of a *Grand Canyon* this can be done by having students read historical accounts which challenge the liberal view of black/white relations that are allegedly constructed outside of the dynamics of power and ideology in the film. *Grand Canyon* may be problematized for the ways in which it covers over forms of cultural self-representation that are constituted within dominant historical, hierarchical, and representational systems. This is not merely a matter of recovering lost historical narratives, it is a pedagogical practice which addresses the issue of how forms of cultural identity are learned in relation to the ordering and structuring of dominant practices of representation. At stake here is not only how representational practices efface the "marks of [their] making" but also how those excluded from the means of representation are actually re-presented (Solomon-Godeau, 1990).

Second, cultural workers must do more than insist on the complicity of representations doing violence to those who are either represented or misrepresented. Cultural workers also refuse the pedagogical practices which support a voyeuristic reception of texts by providing students with a variety of critical methodologies and approaches to understand how issues regarding audience, address, and reception configure within cultural circuits of power to produce particular subject positions and secure specific forms of authority (Grossberg, 1989). In other words cultural workers must make problematic those pedagogical practices that inform particular systems of representation in order to legitimate certain strategies of inclusion and exclusion, practices of subject formation, and the ratification of selective modes of affective investment and expression. Of particular interest here is how particular forms of representation create, mobilize and secure particular desires, that is, how do such representations work as desiring machines to secure particular forms of affective investment. This suggests more than taking up how representations work to police desires, it points more importantly to how students, teachers, and other cultural workers actively produce and mobilize their own desires within particular historical and social contexts as forms of identification and agency.

Third, representations are always produced within cultural limits and theoretical borders, and as such are necessarily implicated in particular economies of truth, value, and power. In relation to these larger axes of power in which all representations are embedded, it is necessary to remind the student: Whose interests are being served by the representations in question in, for example, *Grand Canyon*? Where can we situate such representations ethically and politically with respect to questions of social justice and human freedom? What moral, ethical and ideological principles structure our reactions to such representations?

Turning to the issue of representational pedagogy, I want to argue that such an approach goes beyond analyzing the structuring principles that inform the form and content of the representation of politics; instead, it focuses on how students and others learn to identify, challenge, and re-write such representations. More specifically, it offers students the opportunity to engage pedagogically the means by which representational practices can be portrayed, taken up, and reworked subjectively so as to produce, reinforce, or resist certain forms of cultural representation and self-definition. Central to such a pedagogy is the need for cultural workers to accentuate the mutually reinforcing moments of pedagogy and politics as primary to the practice of representation as an act of resistance and transformation. Richard Kearney (1991) has addressed, in part, this issue by posing the postmodern problematic of representation as an interrelated issue of issue of politics, ethics, and pedagogy. The central question for him is: "how to imagine a set of relations which will do justice to the post-modern imaginary?... to render due account of the complexities of our civilization of images; and to judge it justly according to adequate ethical criteria" (p. 211). In attempting to partially answer Kearney's query, I would propose that a representational pedagogy take up the following issues.

First, this pedagogical approach would give students the opportunity not simply to discover their hidden histories but to recover them. This means "retrieving the betrayed stories of history...through a critical deployment of imagination...able to discriminate between reality as a fact and existence as a possibility" (Kearney, 1991: 215-

216). As part of the pedagogy of cultural representation and identity formation, this would suggest that cultural workers offer students the tools to challenge any notion of subjectivity grounded in a view of history as unchanging, monolithic, or static. Identities are always subject as Stuart Hall points out "to the 'play' of history, culture, and power" (1990, p. 225). Consequently, identities undergo constant transformations.

The relationship between history and identity is a complex one and cannot be reduced to unearthing hidden histories that are then mined for positive images. On the contrary, educators need to understand and develop in their pedagogies how identities are produced differently, how they take up the narratives of the past through the stories and experiences of the present. Understood in these terms, a representational pedagogy is not wedded to the process of narrating an authentic history, but to the dynamics of cultural recovery which involves a rewriting of the relationship between identity and difference through a retelling of the historical past. A representational pedagogy is rooted in making the political more pedagogical by addressing how a critical politics can be developed between a struggle over access to regimes of representation and using them to re-present different identities as part of the reconstruction of democratic public life. Stuart Hall(1988) alludes to this problem as the struggle around positionalities and the struggle for a politics of difference. For him, the important issue here is how a

> politics can be constructed which works with and through difference, which is able to build those forms of solidarity and identification which make common struggle and resistance possible but without suppressing the real heterogeneity of interests and identities, and which can effectively draw the political boundary lines without which political contestation is impossible, without fixing those boundaries for eternity (p. 28).

Second, critical educators need to understand more clearly how to construct a representational pedagogy that is attentive to how the incorporation of the everyday is mobilized within the text of mass culture to produce particular relations between the margins and the centers of power (Grossberg, 1992). In part, this means providing students with the analytical tools to challenge those representations that produce racism, sexism, and colonialism through the legacy of ethnocentric discourses and practices. But more is demanded here than an understanding of the new technologies of representation and how they are used to fix identities within relations of domination and subordination. At issue here is the need to develop pedagogical practices that do more than read off ideologies as they are produced within particular texts. Central to such an approach is understanding how knowledge and desire come together to promote particular forms of cultural production, investments, and counter-narratives that invoke communities of memory that are lived, felt, and interrogated. Critical educators also need to use these technologies as part of a counter-narrative of emancipation in which new visions, spaces, desires, and discourses can be developed that offer students the opportunity for rewriting their own histories differently within rather than outside of the discourse of critical citizenship and cultural democracy. Within this discourse, students would study their own ethnicities, histories, and gain some sense of those complex and diverse cultural locations that have provided them with a sense of voice, place, and identity. In this way, students could be made more attentive to both the struggles that inform their own identities and also to other struggles around culture and voice that often seem to have no relationship to their own lives. I am particularly concerned here about a representational pedagogy that makes whiteness visible as an ethnic category. About making white students understand how their own identities are beyond neither ethnicity, history, privilege, nor struggle. Cultural difference, in this case, must be taken up as a relational issue and not as one that serves to isolate and mark particular groups. This has important pedagogical implications. For example, Bob Suzuki (1991) discovered that in a class he was teaching on multicultural education, many of his white students were ignorant of their own Irish, working class histories. He writes:

> When I asked my students to share what they knew about their ethnic and cultural backgrounds with the rest of the class, students of color-especially African-American students-usually had the most knowledge of their family histories. White ethnic students were generally the least knowledgeable, and after they listened to the long narratives of the students of color, they would be somewhat intimidated and say-sometimes rather forlornly-"I wish I had something to contribute, but I don't know even much about my background. In fact, I don't even have a culture." At first, I found such statements astonishing because I hadn't realized the extent to which ethnic experience has been literally obliterated for many white ethnics. Once I gained that realization, however, I could deal much more effectively with these students. (p. 34)

The representational pedagogy illustrated by Suzuki rejects the notion that the systemic violence of racism and difference as negative identity can only be addressed by focusing on alleged Others. Ethnicity becomes a constantly traversed borderland of differences in which identities are fashioned in relationship to the shifting terrains of history, experience, and power (Hall, 1990). Ethnicity as a representational politics pushes against the boundaries of cultural containment and becomes a site of pedagogical struggle in which the legacies of dominant histories, codes, and relations become unsettled and thus open to being challenged and rewritten. This suggests at the most general level that a representational pedagogy must be a pedagogy of place, that is, it must address the specificities of the experiences, problems, languages, and histories that students and communities rely upon to construct a narrative of collective identity and possible transformation. At the very least, a representational pedagogy must renounce the notion of aesthetic autonomy and fully engage the social and political realities that shape the larger society (Bennett, 1990); moreover, the knowledge, skills, and values that students learn in rewriting the relationship between pedagogy and a representational politics must also be used to constantly interrogate the politics of their own locations, voices, and actions. One pedagogical qualification needs to be made here. A representational pedagogy and politics of representation must do more than promote self-understanding and an understanding of others, it must also work to create the institutional, political, and discursive conditions necessary in which power and privilege are not merely exposed or eliminated but are "consciously rendered reciprocal (and put to good use)" (Khare, 1992: 5).

In conclusion, I want to reiterate that if a representational pedagogy and a pedagogy of representation are to address the challenge of the new cultural racism, they will have to rework the relationship between identity and difference as part of a broader struggle over institutions and ideologies designed to extended and deepen greater forms of political, economic, and cultural democracy. Such a struggle demands a profoundly more sophisticated understanding of how cultural workers can address the productive dynamics of pedagogy within a utopian discourse that can bears witness to representations that narrate cultural legacies which favor emancipatory possibilities, and offer students the opportunity to represent themselves in ways which suggest that they can imagine differently in order to act otherwise. Finally, any attempt to connect the issues of agency, ethical responsibility, and representational pedagogy must work self-consciously within the often overlooked tension between being politically committed and pedagogically wrong. At the very least, this might suggest that any pedagogy of representation and representational pedagogy be rooted in a politics which is simultaneously utopian but always distrustful of itself.

Notes

1 This is not to suggest that questions of identity are not addressed in a progressive way by left cultural critics. On the contrary, writers such as Diana Fuss (1989); Judith Butler (1990); bell hooks (1990), Rutherford (1990); Michele Wallace (1990), Lawrence Grossberg (1992), Stanley Aronowitz (1992) E. Emily Hicks (1991) and too many others to name here are attempting to rethink a politics of identity within a broader conception of cultural difference. But in doing so, many of these critics have failed to address how the construction of identity politics works as part of broader pedagogical discourse to shape popular common sense conceptions of identity, culture, and difference. What is often as stake in this work is exploring the intersection and relationship between different identities, ethnicities, and political experiences within a particular field of domination. What is generally ignored is how these identities are taken up and engaged within particular histories, locations, and zones of everyday life as both a pedagogical and political issue.

2 Examples of this perspective can be found in Berman (1992).

3 I take this distinction from a lecture that Paul Smith delivered on "Clint Eastwood and Being Black" at Miami University in February of 1991.

4 This issue is taken up in Dyer (1988); Hooks (1990); Young (1990).

5 One of the most important analysis of Los Angeles in cultural and political terms can be found in Mike Davis (1990). Of course, in light of the recent uprising, L.A. signifies more than postmodern hybridity, it also signifies, I believe, a "wake up call" to the rest of America. The message seems clear: the economic, political, and social conditions that have come to characterize the inner cities in the last decade cannot continue. L.A. signifies the call for new leadership, new alliances, and the need for massive social, economic, and cultural reforms. But L. A. also makes visible the real legacy of the Reagan/Bush era, one which was aptly characterized by Ralph Nader when asked how he would grade Bush's first term:

> I'd give him an F. All the trends that began under Reagan have
> accelerated under Bush: precipitous economic decline, staggering

deficits, lopsided balance of trade, growing unemployment, declining quality of life, rising personal-income taxes, failing banks, reeling real estate, unaffordable medical costs, fourth-rate schools, rampant street crime, unchecked corporate crime, an ignorant energy policy and abuses of the public trust by a government increasingly unaccountable for its actions-except to big business (Nader cited in Donahue, 1992, p. 10).

5.

Democracy and Difference Under Siege

America 2000 and the Politics of Erasure

For the last ten years, Reagan/Bush conservatives launched a major offensive in both dominating and shaping the debate on education. By eliminating the language of equity and social responsibility and defining teachers in terms that made them appear to be glorified technicians, George Bush and his cohorts attempted to turn the public schools into institutions approximating a mixture of the company store, local Sunday school, and old West Museum. Corporate values, religious sectarianism, and cultural conformity provided the ideological bases for attempting to reprivatize the public schools and turn school policy over to the logic of the marketplace. Within this discourse, excellence became a code word for privileging white flight to the suburbs while simultaneously justifying the poor quality education handed out to students from subordinate groups. In this perspective, high drop out rates, low reading scores, absenteeism, drugs, boredom and student resistance became categories that served as cultural markers to let

Americans know that students who were poor, black, ethnic, or the "devalued other," did not count for much. School failure in the neo-conservative era was defined as a matter of poor character, stigmatized as a poverty of resources and human compassion. Equity became a liberal trick to cheat rich white kids out of an opportunity to get into an ivy league school, and pedagogical authority was invoked as a major policy consideration when the Reagan and Bush administrations talked about troubled schools in urban areas.

During the last decade, schools became the new scapegoat for the increasing failure of the American economy to compete in the new global marketplace. They were reimagined by the neo-conservatives as the new launching pad for injecting into the school curricula the kind of patriotic and commercial fervor that would produce future generations of adults who would shut up and serve in the new army of service sector workers or simply disappear into the ranks of the unemployed and homeless. Schools also became the new centers for character education in which family values, moral fundamentalism, and a Great Book ethic reasserted a nostalgic and mythical view of what it meant to be a citizen in Bush's America. The key terms here were domestic production, moral regulation, and cultural uniformity. The sentiment was elitist and racist. The result was a notion of schooling at odds with educating all students to learn how to govern rather than be governed.

Under the Reagan and Bush administrations, the notion of schooling as a vehicle for social justice and public responsibility was junked for the imperatives of the marketplace and the logic of the carnival ring. Making it in schools became a marriage between trying hard (real individual effort) and being in the right place at the right time (in the suburbs). School reform was defined in terms fashioned out of the language of choice, individualism, and ruthless competition. For Reagan/Bush conservatives, the construction of a New World Order in foreign policy was to be matched by the emergence of a New School Order driven by the ideology of corporate capitalism and the structuring principles of institutionalized racism. The discourse of a multicultural and multiracial democracy had no place in the educational reforms of the Reagan/Bush era. Instead, its guiding reform principles were respect, order, and submission. One of the most ominous results of the conservative reform effort was the emergence of a new racism, which is most evident in the attempt on the part of the Bush Administration's attempt to rewrite the discourse of schooling in the language of vouchers, standardized testing, and self help A central expression of this ideology can be found in the proposed reform document *America 2000*. In what follows, I want to take my chapter I analysis further and examine the ideological underpinnings that structure this document and analyze the implications this logic has for existing and future notions of public education. It is important to note that while *America 2000* may be on hold since the election of Bill Clinton as President of the United States, the ideas that inform this document have, in selected fashion, also been embraced by liberals. Far from dead, the logic that informs *America 2000* will be around for some time, and this makes it all the more imperative to engage these ideas critically and seriously.

Former President George Bush and former Education Secretary Lamar Alexander boldly intervened in the educational debates of the last decade with the launching of *America 2000*. Simply put, the reform proposal incorporates six primary goals and a number of strategies. The goals are of a highly generalized nature and state that, by the year 2000, every child will start school ready to learn, the high school graduation rate will increase to 90 percent, competency will be demonstrated in five core subjects in grades 4, 8, and 12, American students will be ranked first in the world in both math and science, every American adult will be a literate and responsible citizen, and every school will be liberated from drugs and violence.[1] The strategies that inform the document include calls for new national tests and standards, choice based educational policies, creation of a new generation of American schools, initiatives to privatize research and funding for the new American schools, and a limited number of proposals for Presidential awards to both individuals or groups as an incentive for improving academic performance. Unlike any other reform initiative produced during the Reagan era, *America 2000* is a daring attempt on the part of the Bush administration to structure the meaning and purpose of educational policy around a set of values and practices that take as their paradigmatic model the laws and ideology of the marketplace.[2]

I believe that the language of the document lacks a vocabulary for discussing the complex issue of schooling and the future in terms that accentuate rather than diminish the importance of democratic public life. Instead, *America 2000* represents a lamentable withdrawal from what John Dewey called the creation of an articulate public and its attendant concerns with those issues, institutions, and public spheres that are attentive to human suffering, pain, and oppression. I believe that at the heart of the Bush Administration reform initiative is an attempt to remove educational policy from its legacy of public service and to preserve the notion of the public merely as a source of funding for reprivatizing the sphere of public education.[3] Educational policy in this case can be understood as part of a broader effort by conservatives to replace state provision and public service with privatization programs designed to expand the power of capital, individual competitiveness, and corporate autonomy. In effect, *America 2000* puts forward a set of initiatives and principles the aim of which is to not only restructure schools, but also secure a particular view of public authority, social morality, and the future of democratic life.

America 2000 is, in part, an outgrowth of that far-sighted and redoubtable conservative recognition that policy "debates about education have a strategic place within the larger political project. Because education concerns the young, it is an appropriate topic through which to define a preferred future for the society as a whole."[4] More specifically, *America 2000* can be understood as a wider ideological and political attempt by conservatives to divest government service agencies in favor of the private sector, consolidate wealth among affluent groups, and construct a privatized market system which enshrines individualism, self-help, management, and consumerism at the expense of those values which reflect the primacy of the ethical, social, and civic in public life.[5] Many of the major proposals in *America 2000*, including the emphasis on choice, new world standards, testing, and model schools are informed by ideological interests that constitute the demoralizing, grand agenda of opposing social welfare programs, a national health care policy, job training, child care, and programs to eliminate homelessness, an agenda that has dominated American political life since the emergence of the Reagan era in 1980.

America 2000 must also be read as an attempt to rewrite the past from the ideological perspective of a narrow provincialism designed to occlude if not fundamentally elide the historical legacies of previous educational efforts grounded in the discourses of critical democracy, responsible citizenship, and civic compassion that have animated debates about educational policy, theory, and practice for over half a century.[6] Mired in the politics of slogans and catchwords and advertised with a proselytizing fervor that befits the administrative brigades of the New World Order, *America 2000* represents both an attempt to dismantle the reforms of a previous era in which democratic concepts of schooling governed the direction of educational change and a concerted effort to contest the emergence of new public cultures and social movements that have begun to address the increasing problems assailing American society.

As part of an effort to restrict rather than expand the spirit of democratic schooling, *America 2000* substitutes the logic of the market for the principles of democracy, and denigrates or is patronizingly dismissive of cultural difference in favor of cultural homogeneity. Situated in the high tech rivalries of enterprise culture and anchored in the languages of management, accountability, and efficiency, it conveniently forgets the principles of equity and social justice. In doing so, the educational reform program proposed by the Bush Administration serves to undermine the democratic function of public schooling and the vital role it can play in expanding the discourse of citizenship rights and obligations. This is a serious issue and I believe that it can be substantiated not only by analyzing specific proposals put forth in *America 2000*, but also by examining the omissions and silences which equally define the nature and implications of this document for public schooling and the larger society.

Packaging the Future

America 2000 is presented as a "non-partisan educational reform strategy."[7] But the attempt to frame the document's assumptions in the language of consensus and to present it as a national strategy rather than a federal program is betrayed by the way in which it invents the future through a notion of the present and past that is as ideological as it is deeply political. Put simply, *America 2000* weaves a narrative about the future based on a fictionalized notion of the present whose mythical characteristics are neither innocent nor removed from the web of politics and power.[8] In fact, *America 2000* is a deeply ideological and political statement whose interests are, in part, revealed in the selection by the Bush Administration of particular spokespersons to push the reform initiative. Bush's "education team" consisted of millionaire Education Secretary Lamar Alexander whose confirmation hearing was partly delayed because of his associations with Chris Whittle, who pioneered Channel One and is a strong advocate of privatizing school ventures. Another major figure was David Kearns, former CEO of Xerox, who criticized previous educational reformers for not modeling their efforts after the discipline, efficiency, and market values used within the business community. Near the end of his term, President Bush added Diane Ravitch, a prominent critic of multiculturalism and cultural diversity in the curriculum.

The intellectual legacy which informs the work of these government officials is inextricably wedded to the ideologically conservative doctrines of E. D. Hirsch, Chester Finn, Jr., and John E. Chubb and Terry M. Moe.[9] This is not an unimportant consideration since *America 2000* downplays its own ideological interests by forging a notion of leadership which presupposes that the solution to the problems of American schooling lies in the spheres of management and free market economics and that these spheres are unqualifiedly supported by democratic values and politics. The idea that democracy is parasitic on capital gives birth to the presupposition that alluringly undergirds the document: "We already know the direction in which we must go; the *America 2000* strategy will help us get there."[10]

In what follows, I want to focus on some of the main recommendations of *America 2000* and attempt to assess both their strengths and weakness. I will then consider some of the major omissions that characterize this document. Finally, I will provide some general recommendations I think are essential to educational reform in this country.

The Politics of Choice

Reading through *America 2000*, it becomes clear that the perception of what is wrong with schools is one that has been recently echoed by a number of conservative commentators. For instance, economist Thomas Sowell believes that the failing of public schools is measured by statistics which show that "American high school students have now reached an all time low in their verbal scores on the Scholastic Aptitude Test, taken by more than a million young people preparing to go on to college."[11] For Sowell, the reasons for declining test scores rests with teachers who are ill-prepared in the academic subjects, an iron clad tenure system that promotes seniority at the expense of merit pay, and schools of education that spend too much time teaching students about "multiculturalism, environmentalism, and a thousand other world-saving crusades...issues for which neither [students] nor teachers have even the rudiments of competence."[12] Chester Finn has repeatedly argued against local control, and giving power to professional educators and lay governing boards. In Finn's terms, such groups mainly perpetuate their own self-interests and essential abuse rather than wisely utilize whatever power they exercise. Others, like Chubb and Moe, believe that public schools have been pulled in too many directions by the "excess" of democratic demands. While in contrast, "private schools are subject to market forces which encourage responsiveness to their clientele. Their decentralized autonomy, social homogeneity, and strong principles permit them to organize effectively. Thus, they successfully educate their students."[13] These views deeply inform *America 2000*.

Rather than empowering teachers and calling for schools that can act as an integral and positive force in extending a sense of community and neighborhood based on the principle of human dignity, the ideological spirit of theorists such as Sowell, Finn, Chubb and Moe is cultivated in *America 2000*. Instead of promoting local control, expanding the role of public schools in providing community services, and serving as a critical sphere to mobilize parents in building a socially responsible and democratically reciprocal relationship between schools and neighborhoods, the Bush Administration proposal moves in the opposition direction.

Instead of promoting a democratic solidarity and furthering relations based on civic community, *America 2000* offers the American public a deceptive notion of choice that belies a full-fledged commitment to improving the conditions to educate all children by leaving the issue of quality education to the process of moving students from one school to another.[14]   While *America 2000* only briefly mentions choice, it presupposes a definition of the "public schools" that is normative, politically restrictive, and culturally specific and speaks directly to their reprivatization within a marketplace logic. It states: "The power of choice is in the parents' leverage both to change schools and to make change in the schools. The definition of 'public school' should be broadened to include any school that serves the public and is held accountable by a public authority."[15]   Providing public funding for such schools regardless of who runs them reiterates a long-time dream of conservative ideologues like William Bennett, Patrick Buchanan, and Chester Finn.[16] Given the Reagan/Bush Administrations' endless attempts to make choice a central aspect of its educational reform program, this is not an insignificant aspect of its reform initiative.

The Bush Administration's notion of choice is derived from the erroneous assumption that, because it plays a central role in corporate ideology, this narrow conception of choice can be easily transferred to the public sector. Its alleged virtue resides in the magic of promoting competition between schools, and defining achievement solely within the old American virtues of self-help, working hard, and striving to be number one. Choice in this context is both privatized and removed from any notion of serving the public good. Like the corporate, competitive ethic it emulates, it is not about building community and public trust, but about providing conditions for privileged individual students to get ahead without having to question the systematic forms of inequality that make some schools better than others. As part of an effort to reprivatize public schooling, choice simply becomes a code word in this plan to provide public funding for private schools. But more importantly, it offers middle and upper class parents the opportunity to remove their students from schools that are increasingly becoming more ethnically and racially diverse. Choice in this case means more competition, more emphasis on selecting students who will score highly on standardized tests, and more rewards for students who exhibit cultural capital consistent with the "new world standards." Of course, entrance into schools of choice will be based on a notion of excellence that bears little resemblance to equity. What is tragic about this suggestion is that it runs the risk of undermining a public system of free and equal education which is essential in a democracy. Moreover, it diverts attention from the real problems that teachers and students face in schools where there are enormous disparities in per pupil spending. For example, how does choice address the complex problems faced in a state like Massachusetts where per pupil spending in low-income Rowley on the North Shore is $2600 while in Western it is closer to $9000? Commenting on a recent choice plan initiated under Massachusetts Republican, Governor Weld, Jonathan Kozol points out:

> The wealthiest and most mobile families in low-income districts are driving their children to the nearest wealthy district, in which teachers receive higher pay, classes are smaller and supplies are in abundance. Since public money follows the child, and since only those who drive or have to funds to hire drivers can exploit this advantage, the poorest districts are losing their most aggressive, affluent and vocal parents, many of their top-achieving pupils and the public money that goes with them. Low-to middle-income Gloucester, for example, has already lost about $400,000. High-income Manchester-by-the-Sea, just next door to Gloucester, has gained $600,000.[17]

Choice in *America 2000* runs the risk of creating a two-tier system of private and public schools tied to the dictates of a set of "world class standards" that are both reductionistic in terms of their emphasis on measurement as the basis of evaluation, and modes of pedagogy that are defined by the imperative of teaching to the test. Furthermore, its emphasis on standardization suppresses cultural differences in the name of an essentialist notion of both knowledge and teaching. As I mentioned above, even if the notion of choice were limited to public schools systems as it is in some state-initiated school systems, it runs the risks of draining much needed funding from the poorer schools to the more affluent schools as students transfer from the former to the latter.

Of course, *America 2000* is not oblivious to the charge that choice can be used to privilege the rich and the middle class. But its response to such a charge is as shallow as its proposals for implementing the concept. Since a national testing scheme will tell parents how well different schools are doing, it is simply up to the parents to choose the school most appropriate for their child's needs. This liberal notion of choice is similar to the assumption that every American also has the right to choose where to work, sleep, and to live. This is the discourse of Epcot Center. It is totally indifferent to the social, political, and economic constraints forged in hierarchies and webs of power, domination, and difference that limit large segments of the population from obtaining even the most basic forms of economic and symbol capital. The ability to compete, securing mobility, gaining access to information, dealing with bureaucracies, and providing adequate health and food for one's children are not simply resources every family possesses in equal amounts. Without these resources, choices are not so easy since the overwhelming burdens of every day life usually prevent the capacity or possibility for thinking about them or even implementing them. The ideal of impartiality that undergirds the notion of "choice" actually works to universalize a particular version of schooling, one that makes marketplace virtues and the ethics of consumption superordinate to the students for whom such schools are intended to serve. The concept of choice makes sense only if economic, social, and cultural resources are distributed in equitable fashion across all spheres of life, but if this is not the case choice simply becomes another institutional and ideological prop for the wealthy, privileged, and the rich.[18]

Testing and the New Illiteracy

Another major element in *America 2000* is the issue of standards and tests. Allegedly, the six national goals set forth by the President and the nation's governors at the Charlottesville Education Summit in 1989 can be best implemented through developing a set of world class standards in five core subjects (English, mathematics, science, history, and geography). The implementation of a rigorous national (voluntary) program of testing would be used as an index to measure how successfully students were learning in these academic areas. Closely linked to this goal is the creation through private sector of research development money for 535 New American Schools, which will serve as prototypes for the integration of standards and testing.

While *America 2000* calls for more autonomy for local schools, it simultaneously provides model schools, "new American achievement tests," and a National Education Goals Panel to monitor progress regarding how schools reach the six goals outlined by the Bush Administration. While the specific make-up and workings of the NEGP is still being decided, it is clear that the impetus behind these proposals is not only the inclusion of specific subject matter but also the use of standardized tests to set the pedagogical parameters used to monitor progress. In simple terms, this approach not only deskills teachers by pressuring them to teach to the test, it also puts enormous pressure on school systems to adopt a national curriculum , especially if they are to take part in the Bush proposal. The imposition of national testing and a standardized curriculum is not only an attack on the importance of allowing teachers to produce academic materials closely related to the histories, interests, and voices of the students and communities in which the schools are located, it is also a proposal for further demoralizing those groups whose voices have been traditionally excluded from the dominant curriculum. Put bluntly, such a proposal is racist in its implications and represents an assault on the intelligence of teachers and parents and the importance of their role in exercising control over their schools and the curriculum. Within recent years a widespread offensive has been launched on the credibility of standardizing testing.

Not only are such tests being questioned for their exuberant claims for measuring intelligence, knowledge, and skills, there are also growing concerns about how they have been used to produce forms of tracking that are racist, sexist, and class specific in terms of their outcomes.[19]

Issues concerning child poverty, unemployment, illiteracy, health care, sexism, and racist discrimination have been removed from the discourse of educational change. Instead of addressing how these issues impact upon schools, how they undermine how children learn, the current educational reform movement has focused on issues such as testing and choice. In the first instance, testing has become the code word for training educational leaders in the language of management, measurement, and efficiency. Testing has also become the new ideological weapon in developing standardized curricula that ignore cultural diversity, in defining knowledge narrowly in terms of discrete skills and decontextualized bodies of information, and in ruthlessly expunging the language of ethics from the broader purpose of teaching and schooling. The issue of what knowledge is taught, under what conditions, for what purpose, and by whom has become less important than developing precise measuring instruments for tracking students and, increasingly, for disempowering and deskilling teachers.

Accountability in this discourse offers few insights into how schools should prepare students to push against the oppressive boundaries of gender, class, and racial domination, and those dealing with sexual preference. Nor does such a language provide the conditions for students to make visible and interrogate how questions and matters concerning the curriculum are in fact struggles concerning issues of self-identity, culture, power, and history. Similarly, the crisis of schooling is grounded in a refusal to address how particular forms of authority are secured and legitimized at the expense of cultural democracy, critical citizenship, and basic human rights. Refusing to analyze the values that not only frame how authority is constructed but also define leadership as a political and pedagogical practice, neo-conservative educational reformers end up subordinating the discourse of ethics to the rules of management and efficiency. I am not arguing against forms of assessment that enhance the possibility for self and social empowerment among children, forms of assessment that offer new forms of in-

quiry rather than shut down self-esteem and motivation in the name of
failure or humiliation. On the contrary, assessments are important to
get students to reflect on their work and the work of others. But if such
assessments are to be useful they need to be understood within a notion
of schooling that rejects learning as the mastery of discrete skills and
precise bodies of information. Instead, as Vito Perrone has pointed out,
assessment is linked to empowerment when:

> schools and their purposes are defined more broadly,
> and...more powerfully, thought about in terms of dis-
> positions, attitudes, understandings, and knowledge,
> with skills being integral to and not apart from
> them...All of this is to suggest that we need more than
> is now the case to present more articulately a powerful
> vision of schools that is fully democratic, serving all
> children and young people, and rooted in the life of
> important communities.[20]

Teachers as Cyborgs

The most glaring deficiencies in *America 2000* are the strategies and proposals it produces to improve the quality of teaching in this
country. Echoing ideological sentiments that have been put forth by
conservative policy makers for the last fifteen years, the familiar litany
of recommendations appear: differential pay, congressionally-funded
grants for alternative forms of certification for teachers, and the creation of governors' academies for teachers. Given the plethora of recommendations that have been made for improving teacher education,
developing closer links between school of education faculty and teachers in the public schools, and the call for new and innovative ways to
integrate cultural diversity into pedagogical practices, it is surprising
that *America 2000* does not attempt to address some of these reforms
and to build on their best insights. But then again, maybe it is not too
surprising since teachers, principals, and parents have played a very
minor role in providing input into the reform initiatives of the last fifteen years. Of course, the issue is not simply that teachers and admin-

istrators have been left out of the reform movement. Equally important is that fact that there has been little attempt to retheorize both the conditions under which they work and the role that they might play not as technicians but as transformative intellectuals who perform a vital public service in "reviving and maintaining the fabric of our democratic institutions."[21]

There is actually a related issue at work here. *America 2000* like many of the earlier reform initiatives of the Reagan era is rooted in a notion of pedagogy that presupposes that the solution to the problems of American schooling lie in the related spheres of management and efficiency rather than in the realms of values and politics. There appears to be a serious unwillingness characteristic of the Reagan/Bush Administrations to recognize that educational failure is more often than not the result of a social problem rather than a personal or intellectual one. The United States ranks first in child poverty among the industrialized countries of the world. The dropout rate for non-white children in major cities such as New York in some cases exceeds 70 per cent. In Texas, the one hundred top ranked school districts spent an average of $5500 a year per school child while the bottom one hundred spent only $1800. Given the rise of a new underclass among students of color, the spiraling increase in poverty and unemployment, and the emergence of a massive drug culture in our cities, it is both shameful and ludicrous to believe that testing, choice, and the private funding of model schools will address the social context that bears directly on how schools function in this society.

Similarly, teachers are increasingly being asked to adopt pedagogical models dominated by the dictates of technique, implementation, "what works!" and measurement. Concerns centering around learning the meaning of social justice, responsible citizenship, the ethics of care, and the politics of solidarity, and other considerations that do not easily lend themselves to quantitative measurement are either ignored or simply mentioned as a side issue. In part this can be seen in a view of leadership narrowly defined by neo-conservatives as a practice which emulates the style and ideology of leading corporate executives and legitimates training students for the work world as the primary objective of schooling. Hence, former Education Secretary, Lamar

Alexander, endorsed using the knowledge and skills of business leaders to generate the financial resources and ideas necessary to create the prototype for developing 535 schools that will establish the parameters of leadership and pedagogy for administrators and teachers throughout the United States. Lost here are not only those existing models of school reform that have proven quite successful, but also the voices of administrators, teachers, and other cultural workers who have been working on the issue of alternative school reform for decades. Similarly, a central thrust for the current reform movement has been to forge a new alliance between the corporate sector and schools. In this case, the leadership of business becomes synonymous with educational leadership as industry increasingly is called upon to intervene in local schools to provide teachers, advisors, curriculum materials, and other fundamental support and policy-oriented services.   This view of educational leadership is quite paradoxical.   Not only does such an approach to educational reform neglect the discourses of community, solidarity, and the public good. It also draws upon a sector of society that has given the American public the savings and loan scandals, the age of corporate buyouts, the proliferation of "junk" bonds, and made leadership synonymous with greed and avarice.   To be sure, it is precisely the business community that prides itself on abstracting leadership from   ethical responsibility, subordinating basic human needs to the rules of the marketplace, and legitimizing commodification as the highest virtue of American society.

This is not meant to suggest that business has no role to play in educational reform. On the contrary, its role is crucial but it should not be limited to using schools to sell its products or to assuming that the purpose of schooling is simply to act as an adjunct of the corporation in training workers for jobs. Students need workplace skills, but more importantly they need to be able to assess critically the culture of work, to learn the knowledge and skills of citizenship, and to establish themselves as agents who can address the complex and often contra-dictory demands of an increasingly interdependent global environment. This is not merely a philosophical issue, but also a pedagogical issue in which knowledge and power come together to provide students with the conditions that enable them to be critical, ethical agents, to assume a leadership role, to learn how to govern rather than be governed in a world that will demand a new vocabulary and ethics in order to rethink and revitalize the meaning and practice of democracy and community within and across nation states and geographical boundaries.

America 2000 and the Politics of Erasure

In one of the most moving and significant books written about schools in the last decade, Jonathan Kozol has documented how glaring financial disparities in education exist between states, school districts, and even schools throughout this country. Twenty three states presently have cases pending regarding the constitutionality of school financing schemes that privilege rich and middle class communities and decimate schools from poor communities. Hard hit by the current recession, the increasing reduction of funding from corporate taxes, the failure of school systems to pass tax levies, schools in some districts have had to double class sizes, lay off teachers, and eliminate all extracurricular activities. In Oxford, Ohio a private citizens groups had to raise money to keep the after hours school sports program going, but only if students paid a fee for participating. Harold Howe points out that the California school system, once ranked 15th in the nation has slipped to 31st in per-pupil expenditures, "largely as a result of tax limitation laws."[22] The tragedy here is that the students who suffer the most because of the lack of adequate funding from federal, state and local sources are mostly from minority groups, the working class, or newly arrived immigrants. The issue is not merely one of funding, it is also an example of glaring racism. Why was so important an issue simply not addressed in *America 2000*? The notion that 'throwing' money at schools will not solve their problems assumes that schools with overcrowded classrooms, broken toilets, inadequate resources, limited technological resources can function as well as schools who have these resources if only they would become more inventive and resourceful. This sentiment is not only misguided, it is cruel, mean-spirited, and morally irresponsible. This seems especially true after the tragic insurrections that took place in Los Angeles and other major cities after the ill-fated Rodney King verdict. The recent disturbances in L. A. are a "wake up call" that suggests how deep the racial and class divisions are in American society and schools. It is the refusal to deal with these divisions that exposes *America 2000* as a document that benefits the wealthy and the rich rather than those who are struggling for economic and social justice in the United States.

One wonders how many of the architects of *America 2000* send their children to schools lacking in the most basic resources. Or how many of them have read Jonathan Kozol's newest book, *Savage Inequalities*.[23]   In a country in which one out of five children are born into poverty, in which 35 million people lack health insurance, and the cruel plight of the homeless is growing exponentially, the issue is no longer one of 'throwing' money at the poor and disadvantaged, it is one of shifting national and domestic priorities from policies that benefit the rich, corporations, and 'weapons of death' to federal and state programs that provide the conditions for teachers and students in the public schools to believe that their lives matter and that the future of this country depends on the physical and ethical livelihood of future generations. This is not simply an economic issue, it is primarily a political one. It may seem melodramatic but the war is not abroad, it is at home and the devastation it produces through its social and economic policies or the lack of them can be seen in the streets and neighborhoods of every major urban center in this country. What is at stake here is that the issues of national testing, choice, presidential citations for excellence and the development of new American schools do not make a dent in the very real educational problems that plague this country. In fact, the implication that the social, cultural, and economic problems that affect American schools can be "solved by school reforms that require no funding, entail no social or political changes, create no uncomfortable feelings for anyone except teachers and school administrators, and do not touch the structure of a single American institution, including its school system"[24] obscures if not ridicules the very real problems public education faces in the next decade.

The call for rigorous standards and the withdrawal of federal resources for educational reform does not just protect and legitimate established forms of curriculum and those students privileged by the status quo. *America 2000* also represents a direct assault on the issue of cultural difference and attempts by people of color to reorganize the curriculum to include the voices, histories, and experiences of those students who traditionally have been excluded from the dominant school curricula.

What is striking about *America 2000* is that it ignores one of the most important cultural issues in American life: the increasing hybridization of large segments of the population. In light of the waves of new immigration, the growing populations of people of color in major urban areas, and the changing demographics of the labor force and schools in terms of race and ethnicity, it is important to recognize that the politics of *America 2000* simply reproduces the conservative position on multiculturalism which views difference as a deficit rather than as a valuable resource for enriching the tradition of democratic pluralism. In fact, the Reagan/Bush era has been marked by a plethora of books and articles attacking affirmative action and federal aid to minorities while promoting the watering down of civil rights legislation. This has also been a decade in which "the media manipulation of the Willie Horton case...might perhaps be indexed as part of the crest of a tidal wave of racist resurgence during the Reagan ascendancy,"[25] one that has of yet not subsided. Need we look further than the recent candidacy of David Duke for Governor of Louisiana or Patrick Buchanan's bid for the presidency? The Reagan/Bush era has made the term "difference," when associated with Black and Latino populations, synonymous with social degeneracy and criminal violence. While the Clinton administration offers the possibility for tolerance rather than hostility towards people of color, it is important to note that Clinton focused his campaign on the middle class and virtually ignored issued regarding racism.

What is at stake here is whether educators want to endorse monocultural essentialism that pronounces cultural difference and the emergence of multiple cultures as a destabilizing force and precursor to fragmentation and forms of ethnic separation, or do we want to embrace cultural difference as an advance towards democracy. In my view, cultural difference should reject the notion of a narrow nationalism rooted in the mythical identifications of an *a priori* given, common or undifferentiated original culture. But I do not dismiss the important

legacy of our understanding and appreciating national history. Cultural
difference demands that educators take seriously multicultural literacy
as part of a wider historical struggle over cultural democracy and responsible citizenship based on support of basic rights and principles
such as equality, freedom, liberty, justice, and human dignity. Central
to such concerns is the question of who creates the framework for
speaking about issues of tolerance, of diversity, of pluralism. *America
2000* makes it clear that it is not the American people themselves, and
certainly not the oppressed and peripheralized minorities, who should
participate in deciding how the concept of difference or diversity
should be defined and approached. The real crisis in this country is not
about "smoothing over" a supposedly irreconcilable and permanently
divisive identity politics; on the contrary, it is primarily about racism
and intolerance dressed up in nationalist slogans and media sound bytes
exhorting us as new warrior-citizens under the banner of freedom to
sound the clarion call for creating a "common culture." I strongly believe that government emphasis should not be on creating a common
culture but on creating a common ground for dialogue. This has less to
do with developing a uniform and benign melange of cultural groups,
and more to do with establishing the conditions for the growth of a
critical, democratic public culture, one that guarantees basic rights and
entitlements on the one hand, and solicits basic obligations on the
other. It is in the tensional mixture of rights and obligations that a notion of citizenship emerges in which a democratic public culture is affirmed within and across cultural differences. Of primary concern in
this dialectical process is to link social equality and cultural differences
with participatory democracy. At issue here is the task of refusing to
de-ethnicize people of color by insisting that white Anglo-Saxon culture not become the invisible norm that structures the relationship between community and difference. Various groups need to be provided
spaces and opportunities to communicate across lines of cultural, linguistic, class, gender and racial difference so as to affirm their own
voices and to join in solidarity with others who believe in and cherish
critical and democratic public cultures. The curriculum should work to
enhance the possibility for broader forms of solidarity among different
cultural groups. Teachers, students, and parents should be given the

opportunity to be border crossers in order to engage, learn from, and listen to how various ethnic groups negotiate and translate their histories, differences, and voices within and across an over-arching polity. Where, for example, in *America 2000* does it address the importance of bilingual, bicultural programs to provide students proficiency in English while at the same time ensuring their full participation in the specificity of their native language and culture? Where is the support for linguistic minorities? Where, for that matter, is the emphasis on language arts, on literature that would include works by minority authors? Why is the emphasis simply on teaching English? Could this omission point to the existence of a historical society whose roots are so buried in European colonialist discourses that a transparent norm begins to operate that contains cultural difference under the guise of teaching Johnny to read and write? What does it mean if Johnny can write and read in English without learning how to respect cultural difference? Literacy means teaching students in their native languages as well as in English, it means teaching students about the conditions necessary for the production of knowledge and not merely its representation. Similarly, literacy should not be limited to reading, speaking, and writing but also includes understanding how meanings are inscribed through various electronic and visual means, such as television, film, and photography. We live in a world of multiple literacies and understanding them should eliminate ethnocentricism rather than promote it.

America 2000 is a policy which smothers difference in the language of consensus and uniformity. Its basic thrust is assimilationist and its ideology represents a dangerous resurgence of nativism and colonialism in which those marked as the other are denied the opportunity to enter into dialogue with, refigure or perhaps even transform in the interests of a more critical democracy the dominant tradition. While distancing themselves from this view of cultural difference, educators need to take up a view of the citizen that is more pluralized and hybridized than the one upon which current assimilationist politics are built. Concurrently educators need to affirm a notion of multiculturalism which posits a relationship among identity, self-representation, and democracy. Bhikhu Parekh says it as well as anyone and is worth repeating:

> Multiculturalism doesn't simply mean numerical plu-
> rality of different cultures, but rather a community
> which is creating, guaranteeing, encouraging spaces
> within which different communities are able to grow at
> their own pace. At the same time it means creating a
> public space in which these communities are able to
> interact, enrich the existing culture and create a new
> consensual culture in which they recognize reflections
> of their own identity.[26]

The failure of *America 2000* to address the politics and pedagogy of cultural difference suggests an opportunistic agenda based on a
selective forgetfulness. It should be pointed out that the five academic
subjects that form the core of the curriculum also left out the arts and
foreign languages, two subjects marked by the play of diversity and
cultural difference. What is needed is a curriculum of difference, one
that rejects the politics of cultural containment and offers new languages, spaces, and pedagogies for teachers and students to engage in
the process of negotiation and translation around a "third space" in
which cultural hybridity and difference offer new possibilities for producing meaning, representations, and democratic relations.[27]

There is another disturbing silence in *America 2000*. While the
issue of responsible citizenship is mentioned as one of the six goals,
there is no indication in the document how the relationship among
schooling, democracy and citizenship should be taken up by educators.
I would like to make a number of suggestions. I believe that there must
be a revival of linking the purpose and meaning of schooling to creating citizens who can make democracy a real possibility. In part, this
means providing learning conditions both in and out of the school that
develop those social capacities in students in which the struggle for
democracy becomes a primary historical narrative told not just through
the "great documents of rights" but also through the voices of those
groups that have constantly fought throughout history and continue to
make history in the ongoing struggle to expand civil liberties. Students
need to be provided with opportunities for speaking and learning op-

portunities in which they can explore the infinite variety of languages, dialectics, and heritages that make up a more resoundingly hybrid and culturally diverse world than that which existed for the "founding fathers." This would include taking up democracy as part of a broader public struggle waged by African-Americans, Latinos, women, workers, native Americans and others for whom democracy means rendering the state accountable for the welfare of all of its citizens.

Democracy is a terrain of struggle, but the struggle is not limited to restructuring power from elites to various local publics, it is also part of a pedagogical struggle in which conditions can be created for students and others to invest in the debates over the meaning and nature of democracy as both a discourse and critical practice. The struggle over meanings and values is a necessary part of the practice of democracy--a practice that is noisy and agnostic and must escape the allure of a transfiguring coalescence of difference--of difference bonded into a narrative of sameness, consensus, and cultural assimilation.

It is important that critical democracy avoid what David P. Ericson refers to as a "despotic conception of the good."[28] This means that there will always exist more than one conception of social justice and the public good and it is among and across these differences that one can fight the tyranny of master narratives that dictate a totalizing unity of singularity and exclusion, a notion of the state that appears above criticism. Ericson addresses this as a pedagogical issue and I quote him at length:

> Public education should not try to get students to develop a particular conception of the good life. It should not try to bring the student to affirm that (only) certain things have intrinsic value. Rather, public education should help the student develop his or her rationality so that one's political rights and responsibilities are clear and so that one can develop a reasonable view about ultimate issues and ways of life. Public education can best do this through serious curricula dealing with religion, world views, and secular value systems in a critical and responsible manner....And here the curricula

are meant to allow students to explore in a rational manner the various views, theories, and doctrines and their various alleged strengths and weaknesses. Such curricula are also meant to show why these questions and approaches have been taken seriously by others and why the questions still remain worthy of examination. If, as hoped, the student does develop a deeper and more rational approach to life, it will be as a result of his or her exploration and pondering of these ultimate issues, not as a result of being told what to believe and how to believe it. [29]

A number of preconditions for democracy must be established if democracy is not to be reduced to an empty formality in which only a small majority of the population participates. This means social equality and a multiplicity of both competing and complementary discourses must be seen as a basis for political democracy. Additionally, it means that subordinated groups and minorities who suffer degrees of marginalization need to be able to articulate themselves as subjects through their own personal idioms and local struggles and through associations with teachers and intellectuals who are willing to recognize and translate their expertise so that they no longer speak for marginalized others but rather in solidarity with others. Students can also profit from learning how power is mobilized in the interests of reproducing "socio-economic and socio-sexual structures that generate systemic inequalities" [30] and why and how they should work collectively to overcome such structures if responsible citizenship is to become the bedrock of democracy. Citizenship must be redefined as a postmodern concept that does not limit itself to a negative version of freedom, that is, freedom from interference by the state. Students and others need to define freedom as a condition of agency, human compassion, and the ability and willingness to act on choices that expand membership in democratic life, enlarge the domain of rights and duties to include new communities and movements, and to deepen participatory democracy by extending the principles of freedom, equality, and justice to the widest possible range of economic, political, and social spheres. When students and teachers acknowledge that identities and life chances are differentially constituted in relations of power and privilege, relations that speak to issue of class, of race, and of gender, then democracy becomes more than a subject to be learned, an ideology to be internalized, it becomes an experience lived out in concrete work with the poor, with African-American and Latino men and women who occupy the most economically and socially depressed status of all groups in the United States, and with vulnerable minorities like children. It also means learning how to establish conditions and mutual aid networks and working with social movements, elements of a polity that both debate and change policy as part of an attempt to extend rather than restrict the constitutive nature of citizenship.

America 2000 ignores the issue of what it takes for citizenship to become a reality in principle because it does not ground the meaning and purpose of schooling in extending or reconstructing democratic public life. Instead, the challenge for better schooling is linked to better test scores, making the United States number one in world affairs, and educating students to become highly competitive in a changing post-industrial world. These goals may be pragmatic, but only in a very narrow sense; they do little or nothing to further the cause of justice, extend the possibility of human rights, or promote democracy over an unswerving commitment to individualism and the competitive ethic. It is precisely this lack of vision that must be challenged in *America 2000* if the United States and its public schools are to expand the cause of human justice and compassion as a model for education.

In conclusion, *America 2000* is more than a policy document but rather a political spectacle. Good policies provide the parameters for debate and dialogue in ways that enable their underlying presuppositions to be made visible, challenged, and debated under conditions of mutual respect and social responsibility. *America 2000* presents a superficial analysis of and platform for America's schools and parades it under the discourse of goals and strategies which can only make sense by forgetting, repressing, and avoiding the very politics which drives it forward.

Notes

1 *America 2000: An Education Strategy* Washington, D.C.: U.S. Department of Education, 1991), p. 4.

2 The language of the market place amounts to nothing less than an obsession for apologists for the Reagan/Bush administration. Various spokespersons including Chester Finn, Jr., David Kearns, and Dennis Doyle present a view of schooling constrained by a vulgar pragmatism that is notorious for its lack of vision and possibility. Central to this discourse are issues of accountability, testing, standards, competing with the Japanese, educating students for the workplace, reasserting America's competitive edge, and so on. Issues concerning democracy, equity, social justice, collective responsibility, poverty, racism, the destruction of the planet, better working conditions for teachers, empowerment, and other issues that cannot be reduced to the reductionistic, quantitative logic of what works are seen as simply unimportant or ineffective. All of these authors should be read against John Chubb and Terry Moe, *Politics, Markets, and America's Schools* (Washington, D.C., 1990), which could serve as their ideological alter ego. For sources mentioned, see Chester E. Finn, Jr. *We Must Take Charge* (New York: Free Press, 1991); for a concise presentation of the ideological principles that inform Finn's work and its remarkable ideological affinity to *America 2000*, see Chester Finn, Jr., "Questioning 'Cliches' of Education Reform," *Education Week* 25 January, 1989, 30, 29. David T. Kearns and Denis P. Doyle, *Winning the Brain Race: A Bold Plan to Make Our Schools Competitive* (San Francisco: Institute for Contemporary Studies, 1988). Compare the sterile "urgency" of both how the crisis of schooling is defined and responded to by these authors with the works of Jonathan Kozol, who truly functions as a public intellectual attempting to address the relationship between equity and excellence. See most recently, Jonathan Kozol, *Savage Inequalities* (New York: Crown/Random House, 1991).

3 Deborah W. Meier, "Choice Can Save Public Education," *The Nation* (March 4 1991), p. 253.

4 Richard Johnson, "Socialism and Popular Education," *Socialism and Education* vol. 8., No. 1, 1981, p. 8.

5   These issues are taken up in Ann Bastian, Norm Fruchter, Marilyn Gittell, Colin Greer, and Kenneth Haskins, *Choosing Equality: The Case for Democratic Schooling* (Philadelphia: Temple University Press, 1986; Kevin Phillips, *The Politics of the Rich and the Poor* (New York: Harper, 1990); Robert Bellah, et. al. *The Good Society* (New York: Knopf, 1991).

6   For example, see John Dewey, *Democracy and Education.* (New York: Macmillan Co., 1916); John Dewey, *The Public and Its Problems.* (Athens, Ohio: Swallow Press, 1927); Stanley Aronowitz and Henry A. Giroux, *Education Under Siege* (New York: Bergin and Garvey Press, 1985); Henry A. Giroux, *Schooling and the Struggle for Public Life* (Minnesota: University of Minnesota Press, 1988); Lawrence A. Cremin, *Popular Education and Its Discontents* (New York: Harper & Row, 1990); Peter McLaren, *Life in Schools* (New York: Longman, Inc., 1989).

7   *America 2000: An Education Strategy* (Washington, D.C.: U.S. Department of Education, 1991), p. 43.

8   See Harold Howe's commentary on the alleged neutrality posited in *America 2000.* In Harold Howe II, "A Bumpy Ride on Four Trains," *Phi Delta Kappan* (November 1991), pp. 192-203. This is an exemplary critique of *America 2000.*

9   See Finn, Jr. op. cit; Chubb and Moe, op. cit.; and E. D. Hirsch, *Cultural Literacy: What Every American Needs to Know* (Boston: Houghton Mifflin Company, 1987).

10   *America 2000: An Education Strategy* (Washington, D.C.: U.S.Department of Education, 1991), p. 11.

11   Thomas Sowell, "Excuses, excuses," *Forbes* (October 14, 1991), p. 43.

12   Ibid., p. 43.

13   Frances C. Fowler, "The Shocking Ideological Integrity of Chubb and Moe," *Journal of Education* (in press).

14   There is a curious irony here in that during the 1960s and 1970s many whites and conservatives spoke out against busing kids out of their neighborhoods, thus implicitly

at least giving support to such schools. With the advent of choice, voucher programs, and other market oriented schemes, there is almost no protest coming from this groups about bussing their students to schools in other neighborhoods, which in some cases are two hours away from their homes. See Kozol, op. cit.

15 *America 2000*, op. cit., 41.

16 For a ideologically bland, but useful history of some choice schemes in the United States, see Joe Nathan, "Results and Future Prospects of State Efforts to Increase Choice Among Schools," *Phi Delta Kappan*, (June 1987), pp. 746-752. For a critique of the conservative view on choice and schooling, see Stan Karp, "The President's Hidden Curriculum," *Z Magazine* (October 3, 1991), pp. 75-80; Also see Deborah W. Meier, "Choice Can Save Public Education," *The Nation* (March 4, 1991), pp. 253, 266-271. For some reason, conservatives have chosen to highlight Meier's plan as one that deserves both ideological and conservative support. This is not to suggest that choice can only be enacted within a conservative discourse, but that given the way the term has been appropriated by the right, it may take some thoughtful analysis to figure out how to link choice to the issue of equity and democracy in a way that advances rather than restricts the best interests of public schooling for all and not just some children.

17 Jonathan Kozol, "Widening the Gap," *Boston Sunday Globe*, November 3, 1991, A20.

18 Gary Orfield raises some serious questions about how the politics of choice has failed to work in the market. He points to the S & L crisis, the failure of cable TV deregulation, and the failure of free market choice in the Medicaid program. See Gary Orfield, "Choice, Testing, and the Re-Election of a President," in *Voices from the Field: 30 Expert Opinions on America 2000: The Bus Administration Strategy to 'Reinvent' America's Schools.* (Washington, D.C.: William T. Grant Foundation Commission on Work, Family, and Citizenship and Institute for Educational Leadership, 1991), pp. 7-8.

19 Noe Medina and D. Monty Neill, *Fallout From the Testing Explosion: How 100 Million Standardized Exams Undermine Equity and Excellence in America's Public Schools* (Cambridge: National Center for Fair & Open Testing, 1988); James Crouse

and Dale Trusheim, *The Case Against the SAT* (Chicago: University of Chicago Press, 1988); Jeanne Oakes, "The Many Sided Dilemmas of Testing." *Voices from the Field: 30 Expert Opinions on America 2000, The Bush Administration Strategy to "Reinvent" America's Schools.* (Washington, D. C.: William T. Grant Foundation Commission on Work, Family and Citizenship and the Institute for Educational Leadership, 1991), pp. 17-18; Linda Darling-Hammond, "Measuring Schools is Not the Same as Improving Them," *Voices from the Field: 30 Expert Opinions on America 2000, The Bush Administration Strategy to "Reinvent" America's Schools.* (Washington, D. C.: William T. Grant Foundation Commission on Work, Family and Citizenship and the Institute for Educational Leadership, 1991), pp. 15-16.

20   Vito Perrone, "Closing Remarks by Vito Perrone," *Fair Test Examiner* (Summer 1988), p. 9.

21   Deborah W.Meier, "Choice Can Save Public Education," *The Nation* (March 4, 1991), p. 270.

22   Harold Howe, II. "A Bumpy Ride on Four Trains," *Phi Delta Kappan* (November 1991), p. 200.

23   Jonathan Kozol, *Savage Inequalities* (New York: Crown, 1991).

24   Barbara Hernstein-Smith, "Cult-Lit: Hirsch Literacy and the 'National Culture'" *The South Atlantic Quarterly* 89(1), 1990, pp. 82-83.

25   E San Juan, Jr. "The Cult of Ethnicity and the Fetish of Pluralism: A Counterhegemonic Critique," *Cultural Critique* (Spring 1991), p. 215.

26   Homi Bhabha and Bhikhu Parekh, "Identities on Parade: A Conversation," *Marxism Today* (June 1989), p. 4.

27   This is taken up in extensive detail in Henry A. Giroux, *Border Crossings: Cultural Workers and the Politics of Education* (New York: Routledge, 1992). See also Stanley Aronowitz and Henry Giroux, *Postmodern Education: Politics, Culture, and Social Criticism* (Minneapolis: University of Minnesota Press, 1991); Peter McLaren,

(ed). *Postmodernism Postcolonialism, and Pedagogy* (Albert Park, Australia: James Nicholas Publishers, 1992).

[28] David P. Ericson, "Humanization, Democracy, and Political Education," *Studies in Philosophy and Education.* 2(1) (1990), p. 40.

[29] Ericson, op. cit., 39-40.

[30] Nancy Fraser, "Rethinking the Public Sphere: A Contribution to the Critique of Actually Existing Democracy." *Social Text* Nos. 25/26 (1990), p.64.

6.

Language, Power, and Clarity or "Does Plain Prose Cheat?"

> We know that plain prose cheats. (Spivak, 1991, p. 238)

> Accessibility, which is a process, is often taken for a "natural," self-evident state of language. What is perpetuated in its name is a given form of intolerance and an unacknowledged practice of exclusion. Thus, as long as the complexity and difficulty of engaging with the diversely hybrid experiences of heterogeneous contemporary societies are denied and not dealt with, binary thinking continues to mark time while the creative interval is dangerously reduced to non-existence. (Minh-ha, 1991, pp. 228-229).

Within the broader tradition of social criticism, especially as it is being developed in feminist theory, literary studies, art criticism, post-colonial analyses, and Afro-American cultural criticism, a new generation of critics have attempted to unsettle the status quo by refusing the traditional conventions which call for writing in a language that is clear and unambiguous. In part, this approach to writing comes out of the recognition that new ideas often require new terms and that such writing can employ sometimes ambiguous, if not, on occasion, even clumsy formulations. This is more than a technical issue. Rather than suggesting that opaque writing is by default progressive and intellectual (Lowe and Kantor, 1991), a critical approach to writing is, in part, a response to a long tradition of anti-intellectualism in American life in which the call for clarity has been used to attack politically directed writing (Hofstadter, 1963). Moreover, it is a response to a legacy of commentary in which it is argued that such writing is "utopian" and therefore can be dismissed as impractical (Brosio, 1990). Of course, a number of theorists have countered this response by arguing that United States education is supremely impractical from the point of view of its victims (Hooks, 1989; Aronowitz & Giroux, 1985; Giroux, 1992).

Within the last decade, the attack on language has taken a new turn. Now, a strange coalition of conservatives, liberals, and some Marxists have joined together to further argue that clarity is a paramount issue in privileging writing as a form of political and cultural expression. Writers such as Russell Jacoby (1987) have warned "social critics against the danger of yielding to a new Latin, a new scholasticism insulated from the larger public"(p. 236); Ben Agger (1990) suggests that theory itself is to be dismissed because "it courts incomprehensibility" and like much academic writing "fails to invite dialogue, instead reporting itself as an objective account purged of authorial intentionality, perspective, passion" (pp. 35, 37). Susan Peck MacDonald (1990) believes that complicated discourses are the vehicle of what she calls vanguard theories and that such theories are incompatible with the latest findings in readability theories. To prove her point she analyzes the sentence structure and use of terminology of a number of specific writers whose prose fails to pass her readability analysis. One wonders what the differences are between how advertisers use readability tests and MacDonald's view of this particular methodological tool as a practice for creating and legitimating a market for specific products bought and sold either in the marketplace or in the university.

This debate about language, clarity, and experience is increasingly being taken up by a number of educational theorists (Apple, 1988a; Karp, 1991). In what follows, I argue that the recent attacks by a growing number of curriculum theorists on critical educators for using a language that is allegedly "inaccessible" is structured in a binary opposition between clarity and complexity that both trivializes the debate around language while simultaneously contributing to a theory of language that is monolithic, unitary, and Eurocentric (Miedema, 1987; Schrag, 1988; Lowe and Kantor, 1991).[1] In part, I argue that the call for clarity suppresses difference and multiplicity, prevents curriculum theorists and other educators from deconstructing the basis of their own linguistic privilege, and reproduces a populist elitism that serves to deskill educators rather than empower them.

In opposition to this view, I argue for a theory of language that not only recognizes the importance of complexity and difference but also provides the conditions for educators to cross borders, where disparate linguistic, theoretical, and political realities meet as part of an ongoing attempt to engage in a "continual process of negotiation and translation between a series of individual and cultural positions" (Joselet, 1989, p. 123). Finally, I argue that educators and other cultural workers need to take up the issue of language around a politics of difference, one that provides the conditions for teachers, students, and others to learn the knowledge and skills necessary to live in a manner in which they have the opportunity to govern and shape society rather than being consigned to its margins.

Language, Theory, and the Politics of Verification

The politics of clarity has become a central political issue in the debate over the relationship between theory and practice. In part, this position is built on the assumption that critical educators who write in a language that is considered complex perform the double mistake of removing themselves from the public debate about curriculum issues while simultaneously violating an alleged universal standard for linguistic clarity. The most well known advocate of this position is Michael Apple (1983; 1988a). Not only is Apple continually quoted to legitimate this position, he has worked with a number of graduate students who have become strong advocates of the clarity and populist positions (Liston, 1988; Bromley, 1989; Gore, 1990). But Apple's position is not limited to curriculum theorists working in higher education. The call to clarity is also exemplified in a growing number of critical academic and popular journals that appear to define their populist prose against rather than in solidarity with those journals and writers that use a more complex discourse (e.g., *Radical Teacher* and *Rethinking Schools*).[2] The theoretical assumptions that inform the clarity position are stated succinctly in the following comment:

> ....given the overt aim of democracy, the left has to be very careful not to mystify, not to make its claims in a manner that is nearly impossible to verify or clarify. For mystification has had a number of negative effects: It has led to a partial isolation of this work on the borders of scholarship and public debate, and its marginalization has grown because of the arcane quality that characterizes some of the language...the nearly mystical quality of some critical work, its tendency not to take sufficient time to clarify its basic concepts, or to write clearly cannot help but limit its impact. (Apple, 1988a, p. 4)

This argument serves to privilege language according to the degree that it is accessible to a general public and roughly corresponds to an objectively verifiable reality (Liston, 1988). Within this context, empiricism and forms of Western rationalism constitute a strong alliance in the history of critical educational theorizing. Such theorizing is generally based on a reproductive model in which language is assigned the role of critically mediating between the determining force of the economy and the ideological interests capitalism produces and legitimates in different aspects of schooling. Language in this context is privileged for its revealing function, for the ways in which it demystifies how meanings are mobilized in the interests of maintaining economic relations of domination (Bowles and Gintis, 1976; West, 1991). For example, this approach to schooling is often concerned with showing how the hidden curriculum of schooling reproduces the dominant relations of the workplace (Bowles and Gintis, 1976; Apple, 1979), how patriarchal relations articulate between the world of work and the organization of the school labor force, or how the production and circulation of textbooks is largely governed by the principles of political economy (Apple, 1988b).

Within this perspective, language provides a theoretical service in demystifying the means and processes by which capitalist relations organize and shape different aspects of school life. The task of the curriculum theorist in this model is not to question the reproduction thesis as a basic problematic but to show how such a model can be assessed empirically (Liston, 1988). What is crucial to recognize here are the limits that this position places on the very nature of the relationship between language and theory. Theory in this instance is so narrowly defined that it becomes nearly impossible to take it up as a form of writing produced within a language of negotiation and translation that allows an educator or any other theorist to rethink the role that theory might play beyond the task of demystification. In this case, what is lost is the active role that language might play in both producing different theoretical discourses and creating specific social identities. More specifically, the advocates of clarity ignore how language might be used to generate theories that raise new questions, problems, and posit alternative territories of investigation.

The shift in language from its revealing function to its more active role as a productive discourse is also useful in disclosing new forms of domination and in mobilizing new and diverse critical public cultures of resistance and political practice.

Proponents of the discourse of clarity assume that theoretical evidence corresponds to an objectively verifiable reality and the task of the theorist is to unmask such a correspondence. The central role of theory in this sense is generally one of demystification and explanation (Chrichlow, 1991). This is not to imply that questions of validity, verifiability, and explanation should not be important concerns in educational research but to suggest, as does McLaren (in press), that these concerns often mask the deeper ideological, partisan, and political interests behind positivist empiricism and its legitimating claims to scientific method, objectivity and impartiality (Aronowitz, 1990).

As a form of criticism, the discourse of clarity and empiricism fails on a number of counts. First, it is limited to a notion of theory that is confined to a single explanatory account of how schools work and teachers theorize. That is, it situates the process of schooling in a binary opposition between the processes of reproduction versus resistance and in doing so neglects many complex forms of negotiation and translation that transpire within school sites. Tied to the logic of a reactive model, it repeatedly oversimplifies the complexity of social and cultural life and in doing so runs the risk of being overly pessimistic and reductionistic. Second, the assumption that theory only gains currency through its ability to either verify existing practices or empirically unmask how such practices reproduce relations of domination, undermines the role that theory might play in creating new spaces, practices and values. Against the binarism in this position that comfortably pits theory against practice, I argue that both theory and practice are constructed in language and, hence, cannot be portrayed as causally related in which one merely is derivative of the other.

Theory and practice produce rather than reflect their object of reference and as such both must be analyzed as part of a complex politics of representation. There is never, in this case, a simple identity between theory and practice; both exist within a constant and shifting terrain of negotiation that calls into play the connection between the subject of theory and the object of practice (Bhabha, 1988). Theoretical language in this sense is not defined exhaustively by the principles of verification and empiricism, it is also seen as a historical and social construction that actively organizes perception and communication. That is, in this context, theory becomes a form of writing "which does not translate a reality outside itself but, more precisely, allows the emergence of a new reality" (Minh-ha, 1989, p. 22).

In effect, language as a theoretical discourse is neither wedded to a science of empiricism nor to banishing the multiaccentuality of signs as part of a broader attempt to create a singular approach to writing

(Bakhtin, 1981). Language is situated in an ongoing struggle over issues of inclusion and exclusion, meaning and interpretation, and such issues are inextricably related to questions of "power, history, and self-identity" (Mohanty, 1989/90, p. 184). The struggle over language subordinates the issue of clarity and verification to the primacy of politics and ethics. I believe that an emancipatory, self-reflective notion of theory as resistance and struggle offers the possibility for addressing the complexity and necessity for engaging both the limits of existing theoretical languages and the emancipatory possibilities in inventing new discourses in order to analyze the relationship between school, culture, and politics. Ernesto Laclau (1990) is worth quoting on this issue:

> the important epistemological breaks have not occurred when new solutions have been given to old problems, but when a radical change in the ground of the debate strips the old problems of their sense. This is what seems central to me today if one wishes to push forward the political debate....it is necessary to construct a new language-and a new language means...new objects, new problems, new values, and the possibility of discursively constructing new antagonisms and forms of struggle. (1990, p. 162)

But the tendency to exhaust the meaning of theory in the demands of empirical verification does more than strip it of the opportunity to create new educational paradigms; it also generally ignores how theory is constructed out of "those places and spaces we inherit and occupy, which frame our lives in very specific and concrete ways, which are as much a part of our psyches as they're a physical or geographical placement " (Borsa, 1990, p.36). What Joan Borsa is emphasizing is the need for critical educators to turn theory back on itself, to use it to name our own location as educational theorists, "to politicize our space and to question where our particular experiences and practice fit within the articulations and representations that surround us"(Borsa, 1990, p. 36). Theory needs to do more than be stated in a clear language or "express" and verify "reality." It also needs to help educators understand how the politics of their own location carries privileges and secures particular forms of authority. More specifically, there is a strong tendency in the discourse of clarity to ignore questions about the partiality of one's own theoretical language, particularly with respect to the issue of who speaks, under what conditions, and for whom?

Reducing theory to issues of verification and empiricism does not do justice to the issue of the historical connectedness between the language of theory and how it frames its objects. Central to such a concern would be making problematic the significance of speaking from a particular place, such as the university or any other privileged institutional space, and how such a location serves to legitimize the grounds for certain inherited vocabularies (i.e., science, verification, empiricism, etc) while excluding others (i.e., feminism, qualitative inquiry, Afro-American literature, etc.). This issue is particularly relevant for intellectuals who are privileged by virtue of gender, race, and class. It is important to note that such intellectuals reveal traces of colonialism in their emphasis on linguistic clarity without simultaneously critically engaging the way in which Eurocentricism privileges their own position as the guardians of universal linguistic norms, which in this instance serves to suppress rather than encourage a plurality of theoretical discourses and forms of writing (Spivak, 1990; Young, 1990). What is being called into question here is a recognition of the limits posed by the theorist's own biographical, ideological, and geopolitical situatedness. Donna Haraway extends this point by arguing for educators to become more aware that theorists who reduce understanding to verification and language to the issue of clarity are often challenged by discourses that arise out of "partial, locatable, critical knowledges sustaining the possibility of webs of connections called solidarity in politics and shared conversations in epistemology" (Haraway, 1988, p. 584).

Clarity and the Suppression of Difference

The call for clarity by many curriculum theorists represents another side of the debate around the issues of language and theory that rests on a facile opposition between forms of writing that are complex or clear. This binarism is based on the presupposition that the simple invocation to clear language can by itself confer sense. This position also suggests that teachers should be able to engage theoretical treatises effortlessly. Ironically, this position places no burden of responsibility on the reader. Moreover, it also works within a correspondence view of truth which suggests that knowledge is external to language and that the most desirable theories are those that can most clearly "uncover" its secrets through a prose style that best serves as a clear spotlight on "reality".

The imperative to write in clear language redefines the relationship between language and power in largely strategic terms. Allegedly, the tactical value of clear language in mobilizing large numbers of people warrants its use as a preferred element of political discourse and educational writing. This position emphasizes that the value of language is, in part, determined by how people respond to the ways in which curriculum and educational issues are written. Allegedly, the substance of politics becomes inextricably informed by the aesthetics of style. In this case, the advocates of clarity have chosen to largely ignore the question of who speaks, for whom, and under what conditions by shifting their focus to the issue of who listens. Unfortunately, when structured around the binary opposition of clarity versus. complexity, this particular focus on language not only ends up ignoring how multiple audiences read differently it also subverts the very problem it claims to be addressing. Not only does it ignore how difference is written out of language through an essentialist notion of clarity, it also restricts the possibility for expanding public cultures of resistance by refusing to address the importance of developing multiple literacies that allow people to speak across and within cultural differences. Clarity in this case seems to me to do more to create intolerance rather than advance a receptivity to different discourses, languages, and theories.

I believe that the call for curriculum theorists and critical educators to stick to a presumed standard of clarity suffers from a number of crucial flaws. First, the claim that some critical educators write in a language that is arcane and inaccessible reifies the question of clarity in presupposing rather than demonstrating a universal standard for measuring it. For example, do critics who invoke the issue of clarity have a specific standard in mind when they pass judgment on the literacy levels of the various audiences that constitute the readers of theoretical books on curriculum theory and practice? Is it the equivalent of a reading level embodied in *Readers Digest*? What is it about the defining characteristic of their discourse that allows them to judge for *all* readers what is accessible and what is not? Unfortunately, the discourse of clarity appears to rest on a universal standard of literacy that presumably need not be questioned.

This approach to language suppresses questions of context: Who reads what under what conditions? But more importantly, it also strongly suggests that the power of language is defined through a stylized aesthetic of clarity which presupposes the commonsense assumption that language is a transparent medium merely expressing existing facts that need only be laid out in an agreed-upon fashion (Laclau, 1990). Such a position runs the risk of fleeing the politics of culture by situating language outside of history, power, and struggle. While such an anti-theoretical stance may be comforting to some, it provides no help in understanding the complex relationship between either theory and practice or between language and power. The appeal to clarity often ignores how language is produced within particular theoretical paradigms and taken up by diverse audiences across and within widely different cultural spheres. In doing so, it fails to address the complex issue of how languages that challenge traditional educational paradigms are obligated to create new categories in order to reclaim new spaces for resistance, to establish new identities, or to construct new knowledge/power relations.

Second, the advocates of clarity need to be more reflective about the ideologies that inform their own position on language and their ideological construction of the category of "clarity." Understood in these terms, it is important to raise the issue of what makes these academics capable of reading certain educational texts critically while simultaneously suggesting that most educators are not intelligent enough to understand them. For example, in a recent review of Peter McLaren's book, *Life In Schools*, Stan Karp argues that the theoretical portions of the book "are written in dense, academically-inflated prose that makes for tedious reading" ((1991, p. 33). This is a perplexing assertion considering that McLaren's book is an introductory text in social foundations that is written in an academic style very comparable to introductory texts in sociology, cultural studies, political science, or anthropology. The "grass roots" elitism characteristic of Karp's position is not difficult to recognize. What is important to note here is that his elitism cannot be viewed merely as a matter of personal taste, it is part and parcel of a wider ideology in which teachers are called to serve as political activists but are correspondingly viewed as too anti-intellectual and "dumb" to reconstruct the experience of schooling in, and through, a language that is critical, theoretical, and oppositional. Accordingly, this position suggests that activism and intellectual labor are mutually antithetical. Moreover, it legitimizes a position deeply implicated in one of the most powerful ideologies of the dominant culture, a position which invites teachers to deskill themselves while simultaneously serving to place them in positions of subordination.

But such arguments cannot be challenged merely around the hidden ideological constructions that hopelessly shape elitist appeals to the wisdom of clarity, or to attempts to legitimate the alleged self-revelations of classroom "practice" unhampered by the "intrusions" of theory. What seems to me to be the real issue in this discourse is the peculiar form of neo-colonial paranoia which it exhibits, an implicit fear that the world as we know it is a social and historical construction, a world in which language is invented as part of an ongoing transformation of experience, a world that no longer lends itself to simple calls for clarity along with its complementary principles of universality and appeals to the final court of concrete experience (Kincheloe, 1991). In the age of post-colonialism, language has become a terrain of contestation and struggle. It can no longer suppress its complicity in particular forms of violence and oppression by either denying its structuring principles nor can it resist denying a space for historically silenced groups to rewrite their own histories and identities through a different language and set of experiences. The call for clarity incorporates a trace of colonialism in which the search for a unified single standard of writing is tied to the search for a unified identity, politics, and notion of truth. Of course, the problem of clarity is compounded when the universal reference(s) that allegedly informs it is used to buttress a particular version of English. Hence, clarity becomes a code word for an approach to writing that is profoundly Eurocentric in both context and content. Clarity in this case methodologizes language and in doing so removes it from both a politics of representation and from history. (Crowley, 1989).

To argue against these concerns is not meant as a clever exercise intent on merely reversing the relevance of the categories so that theory is prioritized over practice, or abstract language over the language of popcorn imagery. Nor am I merely suggesting that critical educators mount an equally reductionist argument against the use of clear language or the importance of practice. At issue here is the need to both question and reject the reductionism and exclusions that characterize the binary oppositions which inform these overly pragmatic tendencies.

In what follows, I would like to suggest a much different theoretical and political approach to language, one that not only serves to situate my own work but speaks more broadly to the issue of educational criticism and its relationship to the pressing problems around language, knowledge, and power.

Multiple Languages and Democratic Possibilities

> If we lived in a democratic state our language would have to hurtle, fly, curse, and sing, in all the...undeniable and representative and participating voices of everybody here...We would make our language conform to the truth of our many selves and we would make our language lead us into the equality of power that a democratic state must represent. (Jordan, 1987, p. 24)

Implicit in Jordan's remarks is the necessity for educators to recognize how vital linguistic diversity is to cultural democracy. Fundamental to this position is the need to not only recognize how different voices, language, histories and ways of viewing the world are made manifest in different languages and theoretical discourses, but also the need to recognize that some languages exhaust their ability to deal with some problems and issues. This suggest the need for new languages. Put differently, every new paradigm has to create its own language because the old paradigms often produce through their use of language particular forms of knowledge and social relations that serve to legitimate specific relations of power. Oppositional paradigms provide new languages through which it becomes possible to deconstruct and challenge dominant relations of power and knowledge legitimated in traditional forms of discourse. At issue in these oppositional paradigms is the possibility for constructing educational discourses that provide the opportunity for educators to understand and engage differently the world of classroom experience as well as the larger social reality. This opposition often reflects major changes in thinking that are mediated and produced through related shifts in ways of speaking and writing. Oppositional languages are generally unfamiliar, provoking questions and pointing to social relations that will often appear alien and strange to many educators.

What is at stake here is not the issue of "bad" writing, as if writing that is difficult to grapple with has nothing important to say. Rather, the most important point to be addressed by educational theorists is not clarity but whether such writing offers a vision and practice for deepening the possible relations between the discourse of education and the imperatives of a radical, pluralized democracy. Hence, the defining principle for theoretical practice belongs to a "renewed interest in democracy, and...how a democratic culture might be fashioned" (Jay, 1991, 266).

But there is also another issue in the current debate about language and clarity that is often ignored by the advocates of clarity, particularly as it concerns the relationship between language and the notion of domination. It seems to me that those educators who make the call for clear writing synonymous with an attack on certain forms of theorizing have missed the role that the "language of clarity" plays in a dominant culture that cleverly and powerfully uses "clear" and "simplistic" language to systematically undermine and prevent those conditions necessary for a general public to engage at least in rudimentary forms of critical thinking. In effect, what is missed in this analysis is that the homogenization and standardization of language in the mass media, the schools, and other cultural sites point to how language and power often combine to offer the general public and students knowledge and ideologies cleansed of complex discourses or oppositional insights. That critical educators have largely ignored this issue when taking up the question of language makes suspect not only their own claims to clarity, but also the limits of their own political judgments.

A related issue needs to be addressed in this argument. Many educators often assume a notion of audience that is both theoretically simplistic and politically incorrect. It is theoretically simplistic because it assumes that there is one public sphere rather than a number of public spheres characterized by diverse levels of intelligibility and sophistication (Fraser, 1990). Moreover, by suggesting that there is only one audience to whom critical educators speak, there is no latitude for connecting diverse theoretical languages with audiences marked by difference with respect to histories, languages, cultures, or everyday experiences. Such a position flattens the relationship between language and audience and cancels out the necessity of the author/writer to take into consideration the historical, political, and cultural specificity of the audience or audiences that he or she attempts to address. Within this perspective, there is a tendency to perceive members of diverse public cultures as objects rather than subjects, as socially constructed pawns rather than as complex and contradictory human agents who mediate, read, and write the world differently. The politics of such a position often either leads one into the exclusionary territories of Eurocentricism, elitism and colonialism, or into the political dead end of cynicism and despair (Hooks, 1990).

I would argue that language is always constructed with respect to the specificity of the audience it addresses and should not be judged in purely pragmatic terms but also with regard to the viability of the theoretical and political project it articulates. Hence, language cannot remove itself from the "density of specification." It is not the complexity of language, in the most narrow sense, which is at stake but the viability of the theoretical framework that the new language is attempting to constitute and promote. At one level, theorists need to ask questions regarding how language is disciplined, that is, they need to address "the ways in which discourse [is] controlled and delimited: [through]...systems of exclusion, the principles of classification, ordering and distribution, and the rules determining the conditions under which, and by whom, discourse could be deployed" (Crowley, 1989, pp. 1-2). Thus, the real debate over theory and language is about the specific ideological content of various theoretical discourses and how the latter promote specific forms of moral and social regulation as they are expressed in the organization of the school, classroom social relations, the production and distribution of knowledge, and in the relationship between the school and the larger community.

If the language of educational theory is to work in the interest of expanding a democratic curriculum and set of social relations, it is imperative that a theory of language expand the possibility for different ways of writing, reading, speaking, listening, and hearing. The appeal to clarity does not expand the democratic potential of language; on the contrary, educators need to acquire multiple literacies that acknowledge cultural and linguistic difference as the basis for a public philosophy which rejects totalizing theories that view the other as a deficit, or attempt to take "the social and historical processes out of discourse in order to make a certain order of things appear natural and given" (Crowley, 1989, p. 5). What many educators forget is that the importance of language as a theoretical practice is derived, in large part, from its critical and subversive possibilities. Hence, to judge curriculum theory next to the simple yardstick of clarity and "plainspeak" does not offer a serious enough challenge to educational discourses which often attempt to cover their ideological interests through an appeal to universality and the call for a single language. Nor does such a position recognize that support for a single theoretical language shares an ideological affinity with the current conservative demand for a common cultural identity based on forms of exclusion and hierarchy (Aronowitz & Giroux, 1991). Moreover, the language of clarity does not provide the basis for understanding how language has become complicitous with an anti-intellectualism that undermines the ability of administrators and teachers to think in critical and oppositional terms.

I believe that educational theory should be constructed around a number of critical discourses that constantly rewrite, problematize, and construct the nature of our everyday experiences and the objects of our inquiry. As a pedagogical practice, the language of curriculum should provide the ideological and institutional conditions for an ongoing dialogue between teachers, students, and other cultural workers as part of a broader attempt to link schooling with the imperatives of critical citizenship, social justice, and broader reform movements for reconstituting democratic public life (Giroux, 1988). This suggests that any viable language of curriculum must be able to offer educators theoretical and pedagogical opportunities that allow educators to rupture and transform the crippling binary opposition between complexity and language, theory and practice. Fortunately, there are a number of traditions in feminist theory, post-colonial discourse, literary theory, and in the growing traditions of critical and feminist pedagogy that have begun to create alternative projects in which language is being rewritten as part of an effort to redefine the relationship between politics, pedagogy, and collective struggle.[3] While such discourses and practices are always unfinished, they do offer new categories and hope for educators who believe that schools can still be changed and that their individual and collective actions can make a difference in deepening and extending democracy and social justice in the wider society (Giroux, 1988).[4]

Notes

[1] It is worth noting that some of the critics who rail against such language often do so in a prose that suggest their own identities are on trial in dealing with a discourse that is either complicated or points to an opposing theoretical position. For example, Lowe and Kantor (1991) write "much of the writing in this volume is so arcane that it suggests contempt for the reader"(p. 124). Rather than engage seriously the issues raised in the book, Lowe and Kantor sidestep any serious analysis by impugning the motives of the writers. So much for the possibility of serious criticism.

[2] See Karps' (1991) piece in *Radical Teacher*, which appears less as a review than as a policy statement. Also, see *Rethinking Schools'* October/November 1988 issue in which it provides a article on "Critical Pedagogy for Classroom Teaches: A Bibliography"(p. 8). The list acknowledges the requisite gesture towards some of the work of Paulo Freire and then highlights a series of books that are decidedly more prescriptive than theoretical. Most importantly, outside of Paulo Freire and Ira Shor, it excludes any major theoretical work in critical pedagogy published within the last decade.

[3] I analyze these positions in detail in Giroux (1992).

[4] My use of the terms democratic culture and democracy are linked to citizenship understood as a form of self-management constituted in all major economic, social, and cultural spheres of society is more fully developed in chapter one.

Bibliography

Agger, B. *The Decline of Discourse*. Bristol, Pa.: The Falmer Press, 1990.

Apple, Michael. *Education and Power*. New York: Routledge, 1983.

_____. *Ideology and Curriculum*. New York: Routledge, 1979.

_____. Series Editor's Introduction. In D. Liston, *Capitalist Schools*. New York: Routledge, pp. 1-6, 1988.

_____. *Teachers and Texts: A Political Economy of Class and Gender Relations in Education*. New York: Routledge, 1988.

Aronowitz, Stanley and Giroux, H. *Education Under Siege*. New York: Bergin and Garvey, 1985.

_____. *The Politics of Identity*, New York: Routledge, 1992.

_____. and Giroux, H. *Postmodern Education: Culture, Politics and Theory*. Minneapolis: University of Minnesota Press, 1991.

_____. and Henry A. Giroux. *Postmodern Education: Politics, Culture, and Social Criticism*. Minneapolis: U of Minnesota P, 1991.

_____. *Science as Power: Discourse and Ideology in Modern Society*. Minneapolis: University of Minnesota Press, 1990.

Bakhtin, M.M. *The Dialogic Imagination*. Austin: University of Texas Press, 1981.

Bennett, Tony. *Outside Literature*, New York: Routledge, 1990.

_____. "Putting Policy into Cultural Studies." in Grossberg, Nelson, and Treichler (1992): 23-34, 1992.

_____. "Really Useless 'Knowledge': A Political Critique

Berman, Paul, editor. *Debating P.C.: The Controversy over Political Correctness on College Campuses*, New York: Laurel, 1992.

Bhabha, Homi K. "The Commitment to Theory" *New Formations*. 5, 5-22, 1988.

_____ and Parekh, Bhikhu. "Identities on Parade: A Conversation." *Marxism Today*, (June 1989): 2-5.

Borsa, Joan "Freda Khalo: Marginalization and the Critical Female Subject." *Third Text*, 12 (Autumn 1990): 21-40.

_____. "Towards a Politics of Location." *Canadian Woman Studies*, 11(1), 1990: 36-39.

Bowles, S. and Gintis, H. *Schooling in Capitalist America.*   New York: Basic Books, 1976.

Bromley, H. "On Not Taking Literacy Literally." *Journal of Education*, 171(3), 1989: 124-135.

Brosio, R. "Teaching and Learning for Democratic Empowerment: A Critical Evaluation." *Educational Theory*, 40(1) 1990: 69-82.

Butler, Judith *Gender Trouble: Gender and the Subversion of Identity*, New York: Routledge, 1990.

Chambers, Iain. *Border Dialogues: Journeys into Postmodernity.* New York: Routledge, 1990.

Chrichlow, W. "School daze." *Afterimage*, May 1991: 16-17.

Clarke, Stuart Alan "Fear of a Black Planet." *Socialist Review*, 21(3/4) 1991: 37-59.

Collins, Jim. *Uncommon Cultures: Popular Culture and Post-Modernism*. New York: Routledge, 1989.

Copjec, Joan "The Unvermogender Other: Hysteria and Democracy in America." *New Formations*, 14 (Summer 1991): 27-41.

Crowley, T. *Standard English and the Politics of Language*. Urbana: University of Illinois Press, 1989.

Davis, Mike *City of Quartz*, London: Verso, 1990.

Donahue, Deirdre "Nader Rates, Berates Bush in *Playboy*." *USA Today* (May 8): 10.

Dyer, Richard "White." *Screen*, 29(4) 1988: 44-64.

Dyson, Michael "Growing Up Under Fire: *Boyz N the Hood* and the Agony of the Black Man in America." *Tikkun*, 6(5) (November/December 1991): 74-78.

Escoffier, Jeff "The Limits of Multiculturalism." *Socialist Review*, 21(3/4) 1991: 61-73.

Felski, Rita "Feminism, Postmodernism, and the Critique of Modernity." *Cultural Critique*, 13 (Fall 1989): 33-56.

Ferguson, Russell. "Introduction: Invisible Center." Ed. Russell Ferguson, et. al., *Out There: Marginalization and Contemporary Culture*. Cambridge, Mass.: MIT Press, pp. 9-14, 1991.

Fraser, Nancy. "Rethinking the Public Sphere." *Social Text*,   25/26 1990: 56-80.

_____. "The Uses and Abuses of French Discourse   Theories for Feminist Politics." *Theory, Culture, and Society*, 9 1992: 51-71.

Fukuyama, Francis. "The End of History?" *The National Interest*, 16 (Summer 1989): 3-18.

Fuss, Diana   *Essentially Speaking: Feminism, Narrative, and Difference*, New York: Routledge, 1989.

Gilman, Sander L. *Difference and Pathology: Stereotypes of Sexuality, Race, and Madness*, Ithaca: Cornell, 1985.

Gilroy, Paul "One Nation Under a Groove: The Cultural   Politics of 'Race' and Racism in Britain." in Goldberg (1990): 263-282, 1990.

Giroux, H. *Border Crossings: Cultural Workers and the   Politics of Education* New York: Routledge, 1992.

_____. "Paulo Freire and the Politics of Post-Colonialism." *Journal of Advanced Composition*, 12:1 1992: 15-26.

_____. *Schooling and the Struggle for Public   Life*, Minneapolis: University of Minnesota Press, 1988.

Giroux, Henry A. and McLaren, Peter "Media Hegemony: Towards a Critical Pedagogy of Representation." In Schwoch, White, and Reily (1992): xv-xxxiv.

_____ and Roger I. Simon, editors. *Popular Culture, Schooling and Everyday Life*. New York: Bergin and Garvey, 1989.

_____ and David Trend. "Cultural Workers, Pedagogy, and the Politics of Difference: Beyond Cultural Conservatism." *Cultural Studies*, (forthcoming).

Goldberg, Theo, editor. *Anatomy of Racism*, Minneapolis: University of Minnesota Press, 1990.

Gore, J. "What can we do for you! What *can* 'we' do for 'you'? Struggling Over Empowerment in Critical and Feminist Pedagogy." *Educational Foundations*, 4(3) 1990: 5-26.

Graff, Gerald. "Teach the Conflicts." *South Atlantic Quarterly* 89.1 1990: 51-68.

Grossberg, Lawrence. "The Context of Audience and the Politics of Difference." *Australian Journal of Communication* 16 1989: 13-35.

_____. *We Gotta Get Out of This Place: Popular Conservatism and Postmodern Culture*, New York: Routledge, 1992.

Grossberg, Lawrence, Cary Nelson and Paula Treichler, eds. *Cultural Studies*. New York: Routledge, 1991.

Hall, Stuart. "Cultural Identity and Diaspora." in Rutherford: 222-237, 1990.

_____. "Ethnicity: Identity and Difference." *Radical America*, 13(4) 1991: 9-20.

_____. *The Hard Road to Renewal: Thatcherism and the Left* London: Verso, 1991.

_____. "New Ethnicities." *ICA Document 7*, London: ICA 1988: 27-31.

_____ and David Held. "Citizens and Citizenship."   In Hall and Jacques : 173-188, 1990.

_____ and Jacques, Martin, editors. *New Times: The Changing Face of Politics in the 1990s*, London: Verso, 1990.

Haraway, D. "Situated Knowledges: The Science Question in Feminism and the Privilege of Partial Perspective." *Feminist Studies*, 14(3) 1988: 575-599.

Henricksen, Bruce. "Teaching Against the Grain." *Reorientations: Critical Theories and Pedagogies*. Ed. Bruce Henricksen and Thais E. Morgan. Urbana: University of Illinois Press, pp. 28-39, 1990.

Hicks, Emily *Border Writing: The Multidimensional Text*, Minneapolis: University of Minnesota Press, 1991.

Hofstadter, R. *Anti-Intellectualism in American Life*. New York: Vantage Books, 1963.

hooks, b. *Talking back*. Boston: South End Press, 1989.

hooks, b. *Yearnings*. Boston: South End Press, 1990.

Jacoby, R. *The Last Intellectuals: American Culture in the Age of Academe*. New York: Basic Books, 1987.

Jay, G. "The End of 'American' Literature: Toward a Multicultural Practice." *College English*, 53(3) 1991: 264-281.

Johnson, Harold "The Fire This Time." *The National Review* 44(10): 17-18, 1992.

Jordan, J. *On Call*. Boston: South End Press, 1987.

Joselet, D. "Living on the Border." *Art in America*, Dec. 1989: 120-128.

Karp, S. Critical Pedagogy. *Radical Teacher*, Winter 1991: 32-34.

Kaye, Harvey. *The Powers of the Past: Reflections on the Crisis and the Promise of History*. Minneapolis: University of Minnesota Press, 1991.

Kearney, Richard *Poetics of Imagining: From Husserl to Lyotard*, New York: Harper Collins, 1991.

Kermode, Frank "Whose History is Bunk?" *The New York Times Sunday Book Review*, (February 23): 1992.

Kincheloe, J. *Teachers as Researchers: Qualitative Inquiry as a Path to Empowerment*. Bristol, PA.: Falmer Press, 1991.

Kozol, Jonathan *Savage Inequalities*, New York: Crown, 1991.

Krauthammer, Charles "The Real Buchanan is Surfacing." *The Cincinnati Enquirer*, March 3, 1990: A4.

Laclau, E. *New Reflections on the Revolution of our Time*. London: Verso Press, 1990.

Laclau, Ernesto and Chantal Mouffe. *Hegemony and Socialist Strategy*. London: Verso, 1985.

Lipman, Samuel "Redefining Culture and Democracy." *The New Criterion*, 8(4) 1989: 10-18.

Liston, D. *Capitalist Schools*. New York: Routledge, 1988.

Lloyd, David "Race Under Representation." *Oxford Literary Review*, 13(1/2) 1991: 62-94.

Lowe, R. and Harvey Kantor. Review of *Critical Pedagogy, the State and Cultural Struggle* by Henry A. Giroux and Peter McLaren eds. *Educational Studies*. 22(1) 1991: 123-129.

MacDonald, S.P. "The Literary Argument and Its Discursive Conventions." In W. Nash, Ed. *The Writing Scholar: Studies in Academic Discourse*. Newbury Park, CA.: Sage, pp. 31-59, 1990.

Mariani, Phil and Crary, Jonathan, editors, *Discourses: Conversations in Postmodern Art and Culture*, Cambridge: The MIT Press, 1990.

McLaren, P. "Collisions with Otherwise: Travelling Theory and the Politics of Ethnographic Practice." *International Journal of Qualitative Research in Education*. (Forthcoming.)

_____. "Critical Pedagogy: Constructing an Arch of Social Dreaming and a Doorway to Hope." *Journal of Education* 173:1 1991: 9-34.

Miedema, S. "The Theory-Practice Relation in Critical Pedagogy." *Phenomenally and Pedagogy* 5(3), 221-229, 1987.

Minh-ha, Trinh "Documentary Is/Not a Name." *October*, 52 1990: 76-100.

_____. *When the Moon Waxes Red*. New York: Routledge, 1991.

_____. *Women, Native, Other*. Bloomington: Indiana, 1989.

Modleski, Tania. *Feminism Without Women: Culture and Criticism in a 'Postfeminist" Age*. New York: Routledge, pp. 137-140, 1991.

Mohanty, C. (1989/90). "On Race and Voice: Challenges for Liberal Education in the 1990s." *Cultural Critique*,   14 (Winter 1989/90): 5-26.

Philipson, Ilene "What's the Big I.D.? The Politics of the Authentic Self." *Tikkun*, 6(6) 1991: 51-55.

Policar, Alain "Racism and Its Mirror Image." *Telos*, 83   (Spring) 1990: 99-108.

Rosaldo, Renato *Culture and Truth*, Boston: Beacon, 1989.

Rutherford, Jonathan editor, *Identity, Community, Culture, Difference*, London: Lawrence and Wishart, 1990.

Said, Edward "In the Shadow of the West: An Interview with Edward Said." In Mariani and Crary (1990): 93-103, 1990.

Schiller, Herbert *Culture Inc.: The Corporate Take Over of Public Expression*, New York: Oxford University Press, 1989.

Schiller, Herbert *Information and the Crisis Economy*, New   York: Oxford University Press, 1986.

Schneider, Cynthia and Wallis, Brian, editors, *Global   Television*, Cambridge: The MIT Press, 1989.

Schrag, F. Response to Giroux. *Educational Theory* 38(1) 1988: 143-144.

Schwoch, James, White, Mimi, and Reily, Susan *Media Knowledge: Readings in Popular Culture, Pedagogy and Critical Citizenship*, Albany: SUNY Press, 1992.

Simon, Roger I. *Teaching Against the Grain*. New York: Bergin and Garvey, 1992.

Smith, Paul. "Pedagogy and the Popular-Cultural-Commodity-Text." In *Popular Culture, Schooling and Everyday Life*. Eds. Henry A. Giroux & Roger Simon. New York: Bergin and Garvey, 31-46, 1989.

Solomon-Godeau, Abigail *Photography at the Dock: Essays on Photographic History, Institutions,and Practices*, Minneapolis: University of Minnesota Press, 1991.

Spivak, G. "Neocolonialism and the Secret Agent of Knowledge." *Oxford Literary Review* 13(1-2) 1991: 220-251.

Spivak, G. *The Post-Colonial Critic: Interviews, Strategies, Dialogues*. New York: Routledge, 1990.

Suzuki, Bob H. "Unity With Diversity: Easier Said Than Done." *Liberal Education* 77(1): 30-35, 1991.

Taguieff, Pierre-Andre "The New Cultural Racism in France." *Telos*, 83 (Spring) 1990: 109-122.

Tomlinson, John. *Cultural Imperialism*. Baltimore: Johns Hopkins University Press, 1991.

Wallace, Michele. *Invisibility Blues: From Pop to Theory*, London: Verso Press.

Welch, Sharon *A Feminist Ethic of Risk*, Minneapolis: Fortress Press, 1989.

West, Cornell "The New Cultural Politics of Difference." *October*, 53 (Summer) 1990: 93-109.

_____. Theory, Pragmatism, and Politics. In Jonathan   Arac and Barbara Johnson, Eds. *Consequences of Theory*. Baltimore: The Johns Hopkins University Press, pp. 22-38, 1991.

Willis, Ellen "Multiple Identities." *Tikkun*, 6(6) 1991: 58-60.

Winant, Howard "Postmodern Racial Politics in the U.S." *Socialist Review*, 20(1) 1990: 121-145.

Woodward, C. Van "Equal But Separate." *New Republic*, (July 15 & 22): 42-43, 1991.

Young, R. *White Mythologies: Writing History and the   West*. New York, 1990.

Index